MULTIPLE STREAMS OF INSPIRATION

MULTIPLE STREAMS OF INSPIRATION

VOLUME 1

 Enlightening, Empowering, Encouraging, Inspiring

Wimbrey Training Systems

Multiple Streams of Inspiration
Enlightening, Empowering, Encouraging, Inspiring

© 2007 Wimbrey Training Systems

Manufactured in the United States of America

For information, please contact:
Brown Books Publishing Group
16200 North Dallas Parkway, Suite 170
Dallas, Texas 75248
www.brownbooks.com
972-381-0009
A New Era in Publishing™

ISBN-13: 978-1-933285-78-8
ISBN-10: 1-933285-78-8
1 2 3 4 5 6 7 8 9 10

Chapter 1

Mastering the Mind

JOHNNY WIMBREY

Mastering the Mind!
To Master or to Be Mastered, That Is the Question

None of us are immune to adversity, none are immune to temptation, and none are immune to life's trials and tribulations. Whether we'd like to admit it or not, we all fall short in life at one point or another. Every human being will experience the good, the bad, and the ugly. That's a reality of life. The questions are, *what* are you going to do about it, and *when* are you going to do it? In other words:

1. When you get knocked down, how long will you stay there before you decide to get back up?

2. When you receive bad news, how long will you ponder it before you move on?

We may have all come on different ships, but we're in the same boat now. —Martin Luther King, Jr.

3. When you've been broken into pieces, how long will it take before you decide to put yourself back together again?

How Long Will You Decide to Be Mastered Before You Begin to Master?

They say confession is good for the soul, so let me come clean for a second. I, too, have a weakness. Yes, it's true! In the past, and sometimes even now, I struggle and have struggled with lost time. People who are not time-conscious frustrate me. I can't stand to be late, and I hate being unproductive. I value time because it's something that you can never get back. I programmed myself to think that way a long time ago. You may be thinking that it's a good and successful habit—and I agree—but anything you don't master will master you. Although I programmed myself to be a time conscious individual, I never thought to prepare myself for situations that could potentially be out of my control. This is where the problem lies. Good people can make drastically bad decisions when not prepared for an unpredictable change that's out of their control.

You have a very powerful mind that can make anything happen as long as you keep yourself centered. —Dr. Wayne W. Dyer

Some situations may seem very small and trivial to a lot of people, but a lot of small, trivial situations can and do escalate to very regrettable and drastic situations. I remember my first conscious decision to become the master in my personal battle against lost time. It was a beautiful, sunny day in Dallas, Texas, and I was riding in my BMW Z3 roadster with the convertible top down. I was listening to some good music; I was at peace and in the very best of moods. Then, as it happens, I looked up and noticed I had missed my exit. Instantly, I literally began to feel my blood pressure rise. I went from peace to frustration in a matter of seconds. I told you this situation would sound trivial, but you must understand that by the time I got back on course I would have lost at least a whole five or ten minutes. As you read this, you're probably cracking up, but I promise you I am not exaggerating.

What's even funnier is that by this point, I had conducted seminars and self-help courses across the nation, and I had studied numerous different philosophies and personally participated in seminars on self-control. Yet, here I was, frustrated and out of control because I had missed my exit.

As I exited and detoured through some back streets to get back on course, I began to think about something I had recently heard that was still fresh in my mind. "If you want to get over a negative situation, begin to find positive things in your negative situation." So I figured, What the heck? I have nothing else to do; let's see if it works. In the midst of my turmoil and frustration, I began to look for positive things.

My first reaction was that there weren't any, but then I began to look for simple things. I remember it like it was yesterday. As I drove up to a red light, I looked up. A car was passing me, coming from the other direction, and I noticed that the driver was smiling.

I said to myself, if I hadn't missed my exit, I would never have been able to see that person smiling. Instantly, like magic, my frustration went away! Then I thought, man, this is cool. As the light turned green, I noticed that the color wasn't your normal green; it was like a fluorescent, brilliant green. And I thought to myself, that's the prettiest green light I have ever seen. If I hadn't missed my exit, I would never have been able to experience this beautiful green light. Now, I must admit that all of this was totally out of character for me, but it worked. I began to feel excited, almost as if I were in a competition to find positive things. It was fun! I became the master of my own pet peeve. They say a mind is a terrible thing to waste, and I say it's terrible when you don't stretch and exercise yours.

Taking Control and Moving On!

Every individual holds the key to their God-given ability to consciously decide whether to master a situation or be mastered by it. Every individual also has the ability to decide how long he or she chooses to master, or be mastered by, a situation. It is very important that you also understand that every season will and must come to an end.

As I conduct self development training and seminars throughout the nation, it amazes me to find that only 10 percent of most individuals' battles are caused by the situation, and 90 percent are caused by their inability to move on and simply let go. It has always been a personal frustration of mine to watch a person wrestle with a situation that would immediately disappear if they would just simply let it go. It drives me crazy to see an individual be mastered by a stupid situation. There are a lot of great people from whom I purposely distance myself because they choose to be mastered by stupid situations. For example, could a marriage end because two loving individuals don't agree on how the toilet paper should be installed? How could a person be known as a loving wife and mother one moment, and the next moment be booked for murder because of road rage?

Let's be real for a second! Toilet paper has never been the cause of any divorce, and road rage can never be an excuse for any murder. The simple fact is that good people make stupid decisions when they choose to forfeit the right to master an obstacle or an adversity and become mastered by it instead. It is said that you can always measure the character of a man by the size of the obstacle it takes to overcome him. Good people become murderers every day—and good people are murdered every day—because of individuals who simply are not in control of their immediate emotions.

Think about it: How many people do you think are dead or in prison either because of their middle finger or someone else's middle finger? I don't know the answer, but isn't it ridiculous to think that a middle finger could cause an individual's rage to escalate to the point of deadly force? How hard would it be for most people to prepare or train themselves never to allow someone else's physical gestures to control them? What or who has the ability to cause you to lose control and step out of your character? When you hear the words "lose control," it's probably a natural instinct to think of individuals who are literally out of their minds or crazy. We hear phrases such as, "He really went off the deep end this time," "She just lost it," or "He just flipped" all the time. These are extreme examples, but we lose control every day.

No one can make you jealous, angry, vengeful, or greedy—unless you let him. —Napoleon Hill

Individuals who are not conscious of the fact that they are capable of losing control will adopt the habit of losing control. And one who adopts the habit of losing control creates a lifestyle of being out of control. On the other hand, control can be regained. For example, have you ever said, "I can't believe I just said that," or "I apologize for snapping like that"? These are examples of regaining control. Are you conscious of, and willing to recognize, where you seem to be less in control?

When and where do you master, and when and where are you being mastered? I believe if you practice mastering the basics—or what some would call the minor things in life—you are literally positioning yourself to avoid potential disaster. I was once told that you should manage your weaknesses and master your strengths. I'm not saying that we will ever be successful at mastering all of our emotions and every situation, but I am saying that every successful step forward is a step toward being the master instead of being mastered.

Is it possible to be in control in a very intense and heated situation? Absolutely! Let me give you an example. Have you ever seen one of the NFL highlight specials? I mean, like one of those Super Bowl specials without any editing, where you can actually hear what the football players are saying on and off the field. It amazes me to see one 300-pound man hit another 300-pound man on the field, see them slam each other to the ground and lie on top of each other, yelling and screaming insults at one another, while close enough to taste each other's spit. Then when the referee blows his whistle, it's all over; they simply get up and walk away as if it never even happened. How can someone who is so revved up with intense energy and competitive emotions appear to regain complete emotional, physical, and mental control?

The answer is simple. Obedience is better than sacrifice. The players are mentally conditioned by the coaches and staff to understand that the consequences and penalties resulting from uncontrollable behavior are simply not worth the risk. You know what's really crazy? The exact same football player who has the ability and discipline to walk away from someone who's spitting in his face and screaming insults, while slamming him to the ground, gets arrested the next week for being in a bar fight with someone who simply says his team is "sorry." Could this be the same person? Are not the world's legal penalties more severe than the NFL penalties? The real question is, who's coaching you and conditioning you to understand the adversities you will face in the real world, teaching you how to ignore and/or walk away from something that is simply not worth the risk? Is it important to have mentors to coach you in every area of your life? We are the only creation God made that holds the gift of self-will. This means that we all possess the mental capacity to obey or to disobey, to lie or to be honest, to love or to hate, and the mental power to will ourselves to personal victory. If we learn to be the masters of our minds, we will begin to minimize our experiences of being mastered.

Not to have control over the senses is like sailing in a rudderless ship, bound to break to pieces on coming in contact with the very first rock. —Mohandas Karamchand Gandhi

About the Author

Sought after by popular demand by entities all over the world, Johnny Wimbrey's message has encouraged thousands across the globe for greatness.

Johnny is the president, and CEO of **Wimbrey Training Systems**. He has graced the stage with world-famous leaders such as Les Brown, Jim Rohn, Zig Ziglar, and many others. Johnny has been interviewed on national radio and television networks as a young success story because of his incredible life-enhancing messages.

Mr. Wimbrey's best–selling book, *From the Hood to Doing Good* is available in every major bookstore around the world. From homeless, to street drug dealer, to a success phenomenon—Johnny Wimbrey has transformed his "MESS into a MESSAGE" and now encourages the masses around the world to "NEVER let your past determine your future."

For more information, please visit www.johnnywimbrey.com.

Chapter 2

The Man of Her Dreams /
The Woman of His
Livin' It and Lovin' It!

JOEL & KATHY DAVISSON

Successful people have great marriages! You may be wealthy, have a ministry, career, good health, and all kinds of good.

BUT

To be a complete success, you must have a happy marriage.

You know it! You feel it!

Real success does not include living in turmoil with the one you promised to love, honor, and cherish. What has happened since that day YOU said "I do?"

Are You Willing to Learn?

You are on a quest for success. We have great expectations for you.

We may "rattle your cage," but success-minded individuals want it straight.

We can teach you how to have a successful, outrageously happy marriage. An outrageously happy marriage makes life sweet. Sound good?

We Directly Address Husbands

Why? A husband is the "source of life and strength" in the marriage. The Bible word is "head." "Head" does not mean authority or chain of command. "Head" is the source of life or death in the relationship.

Husbands, if you nurture your wives with love, they will overflow with vitality, peace, and joy. They will be well-balanced and wise. If you poison them with death, they will be off-balance, angry, resentful, or teary-eyed. They might be close to certifiable. Either way, **you are the solution to the problem**.

"What About Her?"

Doesn't she have to do her part? Most men think that way. If you commit yourself to being a great husband, she will become a great wife.

Do you want respect from your wife? Do you want the strife to stop? Hey, if this sounds good, read on.

Saved from Adultery and Abuse

We have been living an outrageously happy marriage for twelve years. It wasn't always this way. Our first ten years were painful.

We were pastoring. We had a youth ministry and did street evangelism. In our spare time, we had seven thousand people in a marketing organization.

Our arguments were severe and loud. Joel committed adultery.

Kathy was put on prescribed medication after the adultery came out. We believed in wrong or incorrect paradigms of marriage and we reaped the harvest of ignorance.

New Paradigms of Marriage

In 1994, God began to teach us new paradigms that create outrageously happy marriages. These paradigms work for us and everyone else who embraces them. Take Ken and Christine for example.

Ken was a successful businessman. He owned two restaurants and a growing marketing organization. He spoke publicly three or four times a month and biweekly to a class of six hundred Bible school students.

Ken and Christine fought every weekend for fourteen years! He finally "had enough" of Christine. He was tired of the fighting, yelling, and screaming and she had thrown her last plate at him.

Ken informed Christine of his ongoing affair and well-laid plans to leave her and their five children. He would move across the country to marry the other woman.

You Become the Man That God Has Called You to Be by Becoming the Husband That Your Wife Needs You to Be

Ken read *The Man of Her Dreams/The Woman of His!* We insisted that he created the problems in their relationship. Ken bought the message and accepted the responsibility to initiate positive change.

Two weeks later, Christine was "magically" transformed. Ken's "uncooperative" wife was transformed into "the most wonderful wife in the world." The miracle (of Ken changing) was deep and lasting and they continue to live an outrageously happy marriage. Christine continues to be a true reflection of how Ken is causing her to feel.

Think about it! Your wife helps you by reflecting exactly how you make her feel. Thank God for this. Without that reflection, you would never realize how far you are from being the man that God has called you to be.

Agape and Philandros

Five times the Bible instructs a man to love his wife with unconditional "agape" love. The Bible instructs a wife to respond with "philandros," a warm, friendly, responsive love.

A husband is designed to initiate positive love regardless of his wife's actions. A wife is designed to respond warmly and positively. If a husband chooses to treat his wife unkindly, she is designed to respond in kind. This is his wake-up call. A fool does not accept the wake-up call. He calls her crazy and ignores her antics.

Your desire shall be for your husband. —Genesis 3:16 NKJV

Every woman is born with a gift. This gift is a deep desire for a bonded, one-flesh relationship with her husband. She dreams about her wedding day, which is to be the happiest day of her life.

If you had worked with that desire all along, by making her a priority, listening to her heart, and meeting her needs, you would not be having relationship difficulties in your marriage. What happened?

At some point, your wife felt put down, neglected, or violated. She told you about it. You defended. You justified. Her desire was frustrated. The man to whom she gave her heart was suddenly cold, indifferent, selfish, or even cruel. He probably doesn't realize how he made her feel or how deeply he wounded her. She feels it deeply.

Do you remember how you felt when you were courting your wife? Insecure at times? You thought about her all the time. When she was distant, your heart would drop. You wanted her to love you so badly it hurt.

On your wedding day, her heart turned more intensely toward you. Your heart slowly turned away. You refocused on your next goal, hobby, television, whatever. What did she slowly become? Perhaps just a tag-along who was to support you in all of your "manly" activities in life?

A Tree of Life? Or Heartsick?

Hope deferred makes the heart sick, but when the desire comes, it is a tree of life. —*Proverbs 13:12 NKJV*

When your wife's desire for a bonded, one-flesh relationship is frustrated, her heart becomes sick. Her core being is wounded. When you continually treat your wife great, it is a tree of life to her. She is revived, restored, and strengthened. She is full of life and vitality. She is responding to the life you feed her.

Feed Your Wife's Desire

The Queen of Sheba came to visit King Solomon, bearing gifts.

She came to Jerusalem with a very great retinue, with camels that bore spices, very much gold, and precious stones. —I Kings 10:2

When you fell in love with your wife, you were so excited about the gift she was. She was everything you had hoped for. You worked hard to win her heart and convince her to say "I do." You feed your wife's desire by remembering what a great gift from God she is for you. You "needed" her to marry you. Admit that you need her now. It is the truth. A real man embraces truth.

A Wise Man Listens to His Wife's Heart, All of It

God declared King Solomon to be the wisest man who ever lived.

When she came to Solomon, she spoke with him about all that was in her heart. —I Kings 10:2b NKJV

What does a wise man do differently than most husbands? Solomon made the Queen of Sheba a priority. He LISTENED. He allowed her to share all that was in her heart.

Some husbands cannot listen to their wives for more than five minutes before telling her that she is "really irritating" them. Thus the contrast between the wise and the average husband!

Your Personal Marriage Manual

The desire that God placed in your wife for a great relationship is your personal marriage manual. You read it by listening to her heart.

Your wife knows exactly what you are doing that hurts her feelings. She also knows exactly what is missing in your love for her. She has tried to communicate these things, but you resist her efforts. She is "too needy." Wrong answer. This is not being a wise husband.

Solomon Did Not Resent a Woman's Questions

Now when the queen of Sheba heard of the fame of Solomon . . . she came to test him with hard questions. —I Kings 10:1 NKJV

Notice: hard questions. Some husbands get bothered if a wife asks how his day was!

What Does Wisdom Do?

Solomon answered all her questions. —I Kings 10:3

You're no doubt aghast. You're no doubt thinking, "You're killing me now! Answer all her questions?" That's right. It may feel like it is killing you now, but this is key to a happy marriage. You are laying your life down for your wife by listening to her heart and answering her questions.

Solomon Earned the Queen's Respect by Answering Her Questions

Solomon did not say, "Shut up woman! You show disrespect by asking all of these questions." Wisdom answers! Unwise husbands resent their wives' questions, even the simplest ones.

- Who are you talking to?

- Who is that e-mail written to?

- Who is Lisa? Why did she call you?

- How did work go today?

You answer your cell phone. Your wife hears just enough to know it is a woman's voice. Red flags wave quietly in that marriage manual of her heart.

"Who was on the phone?" she asks.

Instead of maturely answering, "That was Lisa, the supervisor at work. She needed to know where I put the Spillman case files," you say, "Don't worry about it; I have it under control."

Why does a man answer this way? His emotional growth is arrested to the point that he interprets her question as a personal attack or a questioning of his character. He thinks she is disrespecting him. She is not. She wants a bonded, safe, one-flesh relationship. He can't tell the difference!

A One-Flesh Marriage Takes Maturity

What does it do to a wife when her husband evades her questions in this manner? She rightfully feels devalued, dishonored, and put down. You know what happens next, don't you?

"What do you mean, 'You have it under control?' That was a woman's voice. I want to know who it was."

"Back off. I said I have it under control. It doesn't matter who it was. Don't worry about it."

Perhaps he ignores her plea and walks away. Suzy grabs for the phone to check the caller ID. He pulls away. They wrestle for control of the phone.

"I knew you had a girlfriend! Give me that phone! I am going to call her!"

"You are crazy. If you don't back off and quit harassing me, I am going to divorce you. You can't control me like this. Shut up and leave me alone."

She throws a plate at him or kicks him where it counts! Perhaps she crumples in tears and goes crying to the bedroom. Whatever the response, she is a victim of emotional abuse. Her insecure and emotionally arrested husband has no clue what just happened. His conclusion? "That woman is crazy!"

Wrong Solutions

Books written to women offer "wife-fixing" solutions such as "Offer unconditional love, trust, and respect to your man. Your questions convey disrespect and no man wants to be disrespected."

Hogwash! The solution is not for your wife to enable your immaturity. Her job is to help you mature into Christ-likeness (Genesis 2:18) so that you can lay your life down for her, grow up emotionally, and meet her needs (Ephesians 5:25)!

What was this wife's need? To know that the voice on the other end of the phone was not a threat. Her husband's resistance confirmed the worst and all hell broke loose.

The solution is for a husband to be like Solomon. Answer all of your wife's questions.

A Real Man Earns Respect

This is how you EARN her respect. She is receiving life from you. She relaxes in your love and transparency. No real man wants undeserved respect from his wife. Give me a break.

And when the queen of Sheba had seen all the wisdom of Solomon, there was no more spirit in her. —I Kings 10:4 NKJV

When you answer your wife's questions and listen to all of her heart, she finds a place of peace. She will be appreciative of her kind, loving, and understanding husband. The days of fighting will soon be a dim memory.

The Queen Praised Solomon

Your wisdom and prosperity exceed the fame of which I heard. Happy are your servants who hear your wisdom! Because the LORD has loved Israel, He made you king. —1 King 10:7-9

The queen praised him AFTER he listened to her heart and answered all of her questions. He did not buy her the latest "wife-improvement" book. He earned her praise.

She Gave Him Gifts!

Then she gave the king one hundred and twenty talents of gold, spices in great quantity, and precious. —I Kings 10:10-11 NKJV

Women are designed for bonding. A woman responds to a man who listens to her, answers her questions, and makes her a priority. It had better be you, her husband, who is supplying this need! If not, you are in big trouble!

Solomon Gave Gifts

Now King Solomon gave the queen of Sheba all she desired, what-ever she asked. —1 Kings 10:13 NKJV

Here is the pattern:

1. Solomon listened to ALL of her heart and answered ALL of her questions.

2. He earned her respect.

3. She gave him gifts. A wife will give all to a husband who makes her feel loved.

4. The husband gives more; he fulfills her heart's desires.

A pattern for a breathtaking, outrageously happy marriage is now set in place. Both husband and wife are giving and receiving. It starts with a husband, listening, valuing, prioritizing, honoring and answering his wife's questions.

The husband is the initiator. The wife is the responder. A real man **earns** his wife's respect by becoming more like Christ and reflecting His love to her every day. This is real living. This is manhood. A wife cannot help but to admire and respect this man.

Golden Key: Try Living Like a Real Man—Earn Real Respect

About the Authors

Joel and Kathy Davisson have written two life-changing books that teach many new paradigms of marriage, *The Man of Her Dreams/The Woman of His!* and *Livin' It and Lovin' It!* Miracles happen everywhere they are read. Many marriages have also been touched by their live seminars and personal appearances. You can contact Joel and Kathy at joelandkathy@aol.com or by calling 386-206-3128. You can order the books, DVD, and CD sets of these teachings at www.unchainedhearts.com.

Chapter 3

Everything Is Possible

ISRAEL UKOKO

Jesus said, "Everything is possible for him who believes" (Mark 9:23). Many people have heard this statement over and over, and perhaps you have as well, but have you really paused to think about it? Because the more you think about it, the more it draws you in. It forces your mind to wander through the highways of possibilities. It compels you to go where you have never gone before, and to walk where even the brave cannot dare.

Jesus's comment came after a man brought his son to Jesus, hoping to get the boy healed. When the man asked Jesus if it was possible for Him to heal his son, Jesus's reply was, 'If you can'? . . . Everything is possible for him who believes." (Mark 9:23)

Let me illustrate the potency of this statement by sharing a true, modern-day story of a determined boy in Africa whom we will call Michael.

Michael was a very poor African boy who lived in an army barracks with his parents in a big city in western Africa. This barracks shared a border with a prestigious golf course that attracted the finest and the best in the society. A high concrete fence served as security and a boundary between the golf course and the barracks. However, for Michael, this fence was a clear indication of the class separation that existed between his side of the fence and the golf course on the other.

This fence prevented him from viewing what was on the other side, but he soon found a way around this problem. His solution came in the form of a huge almond tree, one of many in the barracks. He would climb up this tree to where he had an unimpeded view of the course and the activities of the golfers.

Every day, he would watch these golfers from the top of this almond tree, a place that had become his secret world. These fine individuals had an air of grace about them that was uncommon, and the way they conducted themselves on the course was an inspiration to Michael. They appeared friendly, polite, calculated, focused, and determined. They had beautiful swings that made the balls travel long distances in the air; it fascinated him, and they were fast, becoming his secret mentors.

All of these golfers had a young boy or girl who carried their bags around the course and helped them find their balls. He later learned they were called caddies. What was amazing was that Michael did not desire to be a caddy. He wanted to be a golfer. Consumed by his desire, his young heart began to dream. He would imagine himself on the course, playing alongside these affluent golfers, and he imagined he was one of them. Something inside told him he could do it. He believed, in spite of the fact that he was devastatingly ill-equipped for the game. His determination seemed to surpass his inadequacies. Virgil, the great Roman poet, said, "They are able who think they are able." Thus, Michael believed he could golf.

He decided to live out his dream. He had no golf club, so he began to practice his swings with a stick. Every time he took a swing, he looked up to see his imaginary ball. Everyone who saw him thought he was mad. After weeks of imaginary balls, Michael decided he was going to get on the golf course to try hitting a proper golf ball with his stick. He told friends of his plans. They tried to talk him out of it, but nothing they said seemed to have any effect on him, as his mind was made up and he was going through with it.

One day, after the golf club had closed and everybody had gone home, Michael jumped over the fence and stood on the very grounds of his dream. He had taken a crucial step in the direction of his goal. Even though he knew he ran the risk of being caught, he did not permit fear to rob him of this moment and opportunity.

As he stood on the tee box, Michael's young heart raced and he looked around to make sure that nobody was in sight. He took in the expanse of the splendor that had only been a distant sight from his side of the fence. Taking a golf ball he had picked up days before, he placed it on the tee, grabbed his stick and took a swing. He missed. Discovering a new truth—that this may be more difficult than it seemed from his tree-top gallery—he laughed. However, he was unrelenting as he took another swing and kept on swinging again and again, until he finally hit the ball. A well of joy rose inside him as he watched the ball take off in the air and land in the middle of the fairway.

With a sense of accomplishment, Michael proudly walked towards his ball and took a second shot and watched it fly high in the air.

Now his joy was almost uncontrollable. He jumped up and screamed, "I can do it! I can do it!"

Satisfied with his achievement for the day, he retired and went home. As he laid on a straw mat on the floor, overwhelmed with joy, he could hardly sleep. He could barely wait for the night to pass so he could return to the course the next day to do it again. Day after day he practiced until he had mastered the art of playing golf with a stick. His commitment and dedication ably echoed the words of Pablo Picasso: "I am always doing that which I cannot do, in order that I may learn how to do it."

One day, as Michael played golf with his stick, a man watched in utter amazement at the skills of this unconventional golfer. The precision and accuracy with which he hit the ball were nothing short of genius. Impressed by what he had seen, this man could only imagine what this boy could do if he had the right tools, so he gave him an iron club to use instead of his stick. Michael was a natural golfer and he took to the club like fish to water. Someone else saw how well he played, and gave him a complete set of golf clubs. Within a very short time, his handicap dropped to 10. It was the great Abraham Lincoln who said: "Whatever you are, be a good one," and Michael was certainly a good golfer.

Everyone wanted to play golf with Michael, not just because he was good at the game, but also because of his attitude. Soon he was playing golf with the same rich and powerful people he had admired and dreamed about from the other side of the fence. He was always polite, and because of his attitude, they showed him favor. No wonder Patricia Neal said: "A strong positive attitude will create more miracles than any wonder drug." These powerful individuals did not treat him with contempt. Neither was he intimidated by their wealth and status. Instead, he was inspired.

Michael was proof positive of the axiom that anything that intimidates you will cause you to shrink, but anything that inspires you will cause you to stretch.

These people did stretch Michael, and taught him valuable life lessons, including the value of education. One of the men with whom he played golf realized that Michael's father was too poor to pay for his education, so he took on the responsibility himself. Michael worked even harder on his education than he did on his golf. He passed his exams and recently received a scholarship to a university in South Africa.

The company Michael kept shaped his destiny. Is your present company positively shaping your destiny? There is tremendous power in positive association, as Michael's case demonstrates. He now has a bright future ahead of him, a future he never would have had, but for the choices he made. All you need to propel yourself in the direction of your destiny is to make one good decision, like Michael did.

Michael's story is one I hope has inspired you, or triggered some positive reaction in you. Faced with obstacles that highlighted his impoverished state, Michael chose to become a victor, not a victim. He rejected failure and chose success instead. By taking the necessary steps, he was granted access into the world of the rich and the privileged, a world that seemed so distant and out of his reach. What was supposed to be a place of shame, became a place of glory, while the place of his weakness became the place of his strength. The place of his intimidation became the place of his inspiration, and the place of his fantasy became the place of his reality. If you confront life with that same attitude, you will eventually emerge a winner.

Like the fence separating Michael from the golf course, there might be a fence that separates you from success right now. What you must do is find a way to pull down any such barriers and cross over to the other side. You must choose to dream big by removing all limitations from your life. Only you can decide how far you want to go; no one can make that choice for you. Abandon the poverty mentality and rise to your full potential. If this poor African boy could do what he did, then certainly you can, too. However, you must be willing to stretch yourself, and venture beyond your comfort zone if you want to become successful.

Many people have gone to their graves with all of their potential buried inside of them. Others are living insignificant lives because they are ignorant of their true identities, an ignorance that confines them to prisons of insignificance and unrealized potential. Do you want to spend the rest of your life in the prison of insignificance? Sadly, many will. Only you can decide whether you want to be a part of that statistic or not. Michael chose to be a star instead of a "loser," and you, too, must make a choice. Were it not for the choices he made, Michael likely would have ended up on the streets selling drugs, in prison, or possibly even dead.

Michael was successful because he found a way to access the company, knowledge, and experience of those he admired. It is axiomatic that knowledge is power. If you receive sound information, you will make sound choices. What are you doing to acquire the knowledge you need to excel in your chosen field? Are you investing in the proper materials to leverage your knowledge? Are you in any training program for self-development? Do you have a good mentor? Do you have a system and a strategy for growth? Remember, life is like a bank account; you can only get out what you put into it.

Success is not a hit-or-miss proposition; achieving success requires a strategic and calculated formula, a secret that very few are willing to share. It is certainly not for the weak or the lazy. Success is for the brave, the bold, and the strong.

Do you have what it takes? I believe you do, but more importantly, and essentially, you must believe it for yourself. If you can believe it, you can receive it. If you can see it, you can be it.

Of course, any dream that is worth chasing will involve hardship and hard work. What you must settle in your heart is that the road to success is a long and hard one. It is full of challenges, and disappointments will be inevitable. However, if you can maintain a positive attitude and keep on pushing, you will make it to the end. I am reminded of the words of Napoleon Bonaparte, who said, "Victory belongs to the most persevering." If you are diligent and persevere in whatever you do, eventually you will succeed.

You must decide that giving up is not an option. You must decide that you will not allow failure, or the fear of failure, to stop you from pursuing your dreams, because your future depends on it. There is a destiny that God has prepared for you and it is waiting for you. The future belongs to those who are actively doing something today in order to better their tomorrow. Now it is up to you to seize the destiny God intended for you.

About the Author

Israel Ukoko "A Minister of Faith"

Israel Ukoko is a man of great faith and integrity with a genuine love for Jesus, the Church, and the unsaved. A pastor, evangelist, prophet, author, husband, and father who walks heavily in his Apostolic call, Israel lives a demonstrative life of faith that captivates, inspires, and transforms those who come in contact with him. He moves with boldness, compassion, power, and authority; healing the sick and driving out devils. Possessing a refreshing and genuine hunger for more of God's presence and power, Israel is a great gift to the body of Christ.

Living in Kent, England, he pastors the dynamic House of Faith Christian Church "Where destiny knows no impossibilities." He teaches, inspires, motivates, challenges, and empowers people to rise beyond the grips of mediocrity to their God-ordained destinies. His ministry is transforming the city, and his church is a part of the burgeoning revival in the UK. Israel and his ministry team operate in healing in a hands-on fashion. Throughout the UK, Italy, African countries, Jamaica, and the United States, they attack sickness with an almost reckless abandon. Legs have been grown out, diseases destroyed, sight restored to the blind, backs healed, and paralysis reversed. Israel has not hoarded the gifts to himself; he has imparted his gifts and taught other pastors to do the same. Preaching and teaching in evangelistic conferences, churches, and mass meetings across the world, Israel has been described as a New General in the Army of Christ, a Pace Setter, and a Pastor of Pastors.

Israel possesses and operates in the spirit of excellence, setting a trend that is unparalleled and unequalled. When asked about the exquisite taste that he brings to the body of Christ, he simply answers "Only the best for Jesus." His heart's desire is to bring glory to the Father in all that he does. As a preacher and an inspirational speaker, he touches both the saved and the secular with the excellence of his faith.

Israel is happily married with two children. He owns a tailoring/fashion designing business "Sanct Ltd," and he is currently writing a book, *Ordinary Just Won't Do*, due to be published in Spring 2007.

Tel/Fax: +44 (0) 1689 890 921; Mob: +44 (0) 7958 981 789

Website: www.israelukoko.com E-mail: israel@israelukoko.com

Chapter 4

Be Adaptable

BOBBY MINOR

A wise man adapts himself to circumstances as water shapes itself to the vessel that contains it. —Anonymous

Popular culture has it that sharks are primitive and stupid. They're just opportunistic hunters, preying on the sick, lame, and unsuspecting, with nary a brain wave—or so goes the popular thinking. And yet, no idea could be more wrongheaded. Under normal conditions, sharks behave with great intelligence, and various experiments have shown their learning capacity compares with that of rats and birds.

Present-day sharks, which exhibit an astonishing range of diversity, have not changed in any substantive way in the last 150 million years (and they have been around for 350 million years), suggesting they have attained a level of evolution that approaches perfection. True, sharks are predators; indeed, with as many as three thousand teeth arranged in five rows, they can be considered the consummate predator. Sharks likewise are incomparable swimmers; the blue shark annually migrates nearly two thousand miles following the Gulf Stream, while the mako shark can hit speeds of 21 miles per hour. Sharks are also prolific breeders. The female blue shark, for example, can give birth to as many as 135 young.

Sharks are also exceptionally adaptable creatures. They now occupy many ecological niches, ranging from tropical seas, to the Arctic and Antarctic oceans. Some sharks even turn up in freshwater streams and rivers. That having been said, sharks, like other highly developed animals have, to adjust progressively to biological change and, as a consequence, need time to adapt to altered environmental conditions.

That is of particular concern today because human modification of the earth potentially threatens the extinction of many species. During the last ten years alone, humans have done more harm to sharks than had been done in the past 150 million years. Throughout their long history, sharks, which survived the age of the dinosaurs unscathed, have never faced such a grave threat to their future existence. And yet, given their track record, you'd have to be inclined to bet on the sharks. Sharks' ability to adapt to changing circumstances is remarkable. One of the leading theories about the extinction of dinosaurs is that a large meteor struck Earth, forcing vast clouds of dust, dirt, and debris into the atmosphere, creating long-term and cataclysmic climate change. While the dinosaur failed to adapt to colder global temperatures, the shark continued to thrive. As Charles Darwin noted in his seminal work, *On the Origin of Species*, "In the survival of favored individuals and races, during the constantly recurring struggle for existence, we see a powerful and ever-acting form of selection." Sharks had what it took to survive. Dinosaurs didn't.

Just as species need to be adaptable to survive long-term, so do individuals and businesses. Those who are unable to adapt end up in the unemployment lines. Legend has it that there was a high profile meeting at the Parker Pens Corporation in the mid-1980s. The company had been successful for a long time, and had done so in the face of considerable and continuous challenges ranging from cheap imports, to widespread availability of cheap ballpoint pens, to the introduction of roller ball pens. Parker, however, had begun to lose its way in the '80s. In an effort to stay profitable, the company emphasized competing in foreign markets at the neglect of its traditional markets. Company leaders realized the strategy was failing and arranged a strategic meeting. Just one item was on the agenda: "What market are we in?" The answer transformed the business and reinvigorated it with life.

One learns to itch where one can scratch. —Ernest Bramah

Someone at the meeting asked a simple yet poignant question, "When did you last receive a Parker pen?" Think about that yourself. Most likely, you'll have an answer similar to those that arose at the Parker meeting. You received one as a birthday or Christmas present, or as part of a presentation. It was a reward of some sort. Company leaders realized that Parker was in the gift business. As such, it made no sense for the company to attempt to compete with makers of cheap, throwaway pens. As a result, the company abandoned a strategy of continually cutting costs and quality. The company actually spent more, and redesigned and repackaged their products. The advertising budget was increased by 60 percent.

Parker raised prices and began to target the "style-conscious and affluent sector." Despite a world recession, Parker Pens increased its turnover by almost 50 percent in the last half of the decade.

As the Parker Pens story illustrates, sometimes adaptability means staying the course and focusing on the things that made us successful to begin with. Of course, it also means that if we find we're gaining no traction in our attempt to stay competitive, we need to be nimble enough to switch gears and try another tack. Indeed, Parker originally thought it was being adaptable when it responded to an influx of cheap pens by cutting costs and quality. But people weren't buying Parker pens to stock the company supply cabinet. Recognizing that fact returned the company to its roots and infused its revival with phenomenal success in a down market. The story illustrates the necessity of determining your market style.

According to Jonas Ridderstale and Kjell Nordstrom, authors of *Karaoke Capitalism*, markets can be termed either "fit" or "sexy." They argue that companies like Hewlett-Packard and 3M are fit because they are highly adaptable, continually changing, and ever on the lookout for new opportunities. By contrast, companies such as Ferrari and Parker Pens, market leaders in niche markets, are sexy. For sexy companies, attempting to adapt to changing conditions can be death, as Parker nearly learned. Even some of the seemingly immortal companies such as US Airways, Polaroid, Enron, and K mart, have declined or disappeared in recent years—evidence of a trend of declining lifespan for companies. In the 1930s, the average lifespan of companies was more than 60 years. Today, it is just 12.5 years.

Does this declining lifespan mean that companies today are failures? Not necessarily. Consider the remarks of paleontologist and environmentalist Ed Rose, who wrote: "We tend to think of extinction as a mark of failure—as something that happens to a species that is somehow not up to the challenge that nature presents to it. In fact, extinction appears to be the ultimate fate of all species: more than 99.9 percent of all the species that ever existed are now extinct—probably as much a result of bad luck as of bad genes." Rose's observation appears to be as true for organizations as it is for plants, animals, and people. And if extinction is unavoidable, perhaps some of the lessons of nature can be applied to business to help delay the inevitable for as long as possible.

If you live in the river you should make friends with the crocodile.
—*Indian Proverb*

For my money, if there ever were a "fit," adaptable species to copy, sharks would be it. In Darwinian terms, they are the epitome of natural selection. They have roamed the world's waters for some 350 million years, and have survived by adapting to different challenges and changing environments. They survive in a wide variety of conditions, and live through a vast range of temperatures and hosts of challenges.

One interesting biological fact about sharks bears emulation: Sharks must keep moving or they will die. It seems to me that 3M is about as close to a shark as we can find in the contemporary business world. This $20 billion company has proved incredibly adaptable through the years. The 3M company began in 1902 as the Minnesota Mining and Manufacturing Company, and primarily was a concern that mined for material to make sandpaper. Throughout the next one hundred years the company changed and evolved. Today, its offerings include sandpaper, Scotch tape, magnetic tape, microfilm, overhead projectors, Post-it notes, respirators, pharmaceuticals, and high-tech products. Clearly, 3M is a company that knows how to change and adapt. That ability, however, is not an accident or a quirk of nature. The company has research laboratories in thirty-one countries outside of the United States and more than twenty-six hundred employees dedicated to research and development.

> *To the man who only has a hammer in the toolkit, every problem looks like a nail. —Abraham H. Maslow*

Fit companies are contrasted with "sexy" companies. In nature, sexy animals survive even though logic would dictate that they fall by the wayside as more fit animals dominate the reproduction landscape. And yet, we see examples all the time of unfit animals thriving.

Consider the peacock. It clearly isn't designed for survival. Its tail is too long and it is not suited to flying. Its very existence appears to fly in the face of natural selection, which concerns itself with the survival of the fittest—the notion that the stronger, more clever animals pass on their genes through a variety of strategies. It survives, however, because it is sexy. Females choose these flashy males with the dubious long tails based upon looks. Peacocks appear to know this, spending about 15 percent of their day preening and keeping themselves sexy—roughly four times as long as the female.

In a related manner, there are companies that work hard at staying sexy and making it appear effortless. BMW, for example, employs more than one hundred people in its accoustics and vibration technology departments. These employees make sure that everything from the sound of the windshield wipers to the sound doors make when closing is acoustically perfect. Computer simulator designer Christian Muhldorfer described the sound of a new development model thus, "The door now has a full, reassuring feel." BMW, like peacocks, obviously works hard to be sexy.

One need not look far, however, to see examples of companies that suffer when they begin to take their success for granted. For example, Encyclopedia Britannica believed it had an invincible worldwide niche. Sales in 1990 reached $650 million. But when technological advances came along, Encyclopedia Britannica ignored them and failed to effectively adapt. By 1996, sales had dropped to $325 million and Jacob Safra, a Swiss businessman, was able to buy the company for a fraction of its book value. Similarly, Polaroid resisted technology's march. Sounding like the buggy whip manufacturer at the dawn of the automobile era, Polaroid CEO Gary Dicamillo in a 1998 Harvard Business School profile said, "Some people think photography is going to go away as everything in our industry becomes digitized. But I disagree. I think analog photography will endure." Three years later, Polaroid filed for bankruptcy with nearly $1 billion in debts.

There are few successful peacocks around in business. You'll find them clustered in the luxury market. Every other company, however, needs to be adaptable, flexible, and in constant motion. Of course, they need to keep moving in the right direction. For example, the pressures being placed on McDonald's to produce healthy fare options would appear to put pressure on them to adapt. There is a real danger that McDonald's could alienate its traditional consumers while simultaneously failing to attract health-conscious eaters. Frankly, if you're searching for a healthy option, McDonald's wouldn't be the first name to leap to mind. Even the sexy peacocks of the business world must keep moving, however. They must constantly work to do everything they can to retain their sexy image.

This seems a straightforward, common sense approach. And yet, it is problematic for some businesses. Take the case of Walt Disney, a company that could be the very definition of a sexy company. With a household name and a positive reputation built up over the course of eighty years, Disney is unique. Unfortunately for Disney, the company has been in clear decline over the past decade. To outsiders it appears that Disney has been trying to adapt and pull in a broader audience, and in so doing, has lost one of its unique, core values—its commitment to families and family values. When you hear Roy Disney describe the company his father and uncle established as being "rapacious, soulless, and always looking for the quick buck," you know you're in trouble.

I found out that if you are going to win games, you had better be ready to adapt. —Scotty Bowman

Clearly, to be successful, companies and individuals need to identify whether they are fit or sexy. Even then, however, there will be no substitute for hard work and constant questioning about what market you serve. The key, in short, is adaptability.

When asked to develop an article on effective leadership, Ed Rose came up with one of the finest descriptions you'll ever find. Rose candidly admits that as a young manager, he fell into the "traditional leader" model of management that worked so well for him on the mean New Jersey streets of his youth. In essence, this management style asserts top-down power; you do what the boss says or else. It was not until many years later that Rose began to question the long-term effectiveness of such a style. The more he questioned, the more he came to realize that there are, in fact, better and more effective management styles, and that they had been available to any student of history.

For example, a seventeenth century Russian field marshal named Count Suvorov never lost a battle, even when outnumbered. His secret? Suvorov realized that the foot soldier was the engine of his success. He treated them with respect, trained them to be skillful, and encouraged them to greatness. So why have so many generations of leaders failed to learn from Suvorov's success? "To learn from the past we must have 'paradigm flexibility,'" Rose said. "We have to remain adaptable and not get ourselves locked into having only one way to do something." He noted that the opposite condition is "paradigm paralysis," in which you limit yourself to one fixed thought or context. Summing up, he said, "Simply said, a leader must be adaptable."

According to Rose, the leader who can gain the trust of his followers will likewise earn their commitment and respect. Moreover, committed people will follow their leaders absolutely anywhere. Leaders such as Suvorov, Rose said, had: ". . . learned the importance of their followers being resourceful, and they recognized the need of providing training in the areas that would help them make better decisions and be more effective in action. They also realized the need for their followers to maintain an optimistic outlook, which required the leader to establish a positive vision of the future, either for them, their family, or their country. Finally, through their actions, these leaders demonstrated consideration for their followers by being committed to excellence."

Rose's foray into the attributes of effective leaders led him to formulate a summary of traits that are "musts" for strong leadership. The first is adaptability. Noting that Charles Darwin found that successful species are the ones most responsive to change, Rose said, "Leaders must be adaptable to change." There's no use, he argued, in keeping a tradition that creates roadblocks to progress and success. As we strive to reach our dreams, we must be willing to allow ourselves to adapt to changing conditions. The alternative is extinction. Be the shark, not the dinosaur.

About the Author

Utilizing lessons and skills he learned on the streets, Bobby Minor catapulted himself to success in corporate America. From a first job reading meters for a utility company, Bobby went on to achieve phenomenal success in sales.

Driven by his dreams, Bobby wowed Fortune 500 companies with his hustle and can-do spirit, earning top salesman status. Along the way, he also helped large companies enter profitable new ventures by identifying new niche markets and developing successful plans to exploit them.

This experience ignited an entrepreneurial fire within him, and Bobby eventually went on to found several highly successful specialty publications, even though he had no previous experience in publishing.

Today, Bobby is the author of the book, *Dream Big, Win Big!—Discover the Champion Within You by Changing the Way You Think*, and helps others achieve their dreams through a full-time consulting and public speaking business. He has shared the stage with the likes of Les Brown, Zig Ziglar, and Johnny Wimbrey. Using his proven methods of success, Bobby is helping thousands of people achieve the life of their dreams, by showing them that if they dream big, they can win big. Bobby is a lifelong resident of Fort Worth, Texas, and is happily married to Cary. He enjoys the rigors and joys of being father to Caleb, Carimar, and Julian, and is active in his church, Waves of Faith.

For more information, please visit www.bobbyminor.com or www.lifecanchange.com.

Chapter 5

What Do You Want?

ROCHELLE OWENS

Having a dream gives people a reason to live. A dream is a vision of a hope or an aspiration; something we want to achieve. Dreaming gives us the answer to the age-old question, "What do we want?" Not knowing what we want causes us to drift aimlessly through life. Young people often use the word "whatever," demonstrating a level of ambivalence that is instructive. The "whatever" attitude is what life is like without a dream. When you want something specific, it stirs a cause and effect action.

I have children and a background of working with children in a professional setting. I often heard them talk about what they wanted to be when they grew up. It was usually something like a fireman, doctor, or teacher, just to name a few. In their precious minds, that was what they wanted and believed they could do.

Of course, as we grow, our sense of the possible changes because we gain more knowledge and experience life at different levels. So the answer to the question of what you want now may not be what it was when you were a child. Why? A few things may have happened: (1) You may have forgotten how to dream; (2) You may have shared your dream with someone who shot it down; (3) You may have never believed your dream was achievable; or (4) You may not know what you want.

I have found that, when people believe they can accomplish something, no one is able to convince them otherwise. Les Brown, Michael Jordan, Oprah Winfrey, Helen Baylor, Lance Armstrong, and Robert T. Kiyosaki, for example, had dreams and brought them to life. When reading their stories, one is struck by how difficult their journeys were, especially given that there were people along their paths who did not believe they could reach such phenomenal goals. However, they did not allow the "dream crushers" to destroy what *they wanted to accomplish*!

The key was that they knew exactly what they wanted. In my late teens, I experienced what it was like to not know what I wanted. I applied for a job at a bank in downtown Chicago. During the interview, I was asked what type of work I wanted to do. The only answer I had was that I wanted a job. Guess what? You got it: I did not get the job. I walked away hurt and disappointed, but it was not the end of the world. In fact, I learned a good lesson. I began to think about what I wanted and why I wanted it.

As a child, and even to this day, people try to slam my dreams. I refuse to let anyone destroy my view of my life. It's all about knowing *what you want*, believing in yourself and making a decision.

If we look into our heart and soul, we can find that thing for which we have a passion. Once we find it, we'll find that we're able to visualize and articulate what it is we want. God's Word says in Philippians 1:6 that "he who began a good work in you will carry it on to completion." That does not mean that God is going to do it for us, but that He is there to help us. Our job is to have the faith to work the dream. Yes, there will be obstacles, fear, failure, and people who love you trying to stop you out of love (their own fear). Others will try to stop you because they are just plain old dream crushers. If we have truly found our passion and believe in the God who lives within us, we will have the confidence to find a way to persevere and develop our dream. God is so awesome that He always has what we need in place to help us to the next level. My point is that we should not worry about what we do not have. We need to work with what God has given us, and the rest will come.

I attended a high school graduation recently, and the valedictorian stated in her speech that there were only two ways to get out of her neighborhood—death or an education. She chose college as her way out. That was what she wanted. I can imagine this was a challenge, but she had a plan and she worked that plan to beat the odds. This young lady will go far, because she has dreams beyond high school graduation. By getting out, she knows it's not over, but she has decided to take that journey to build a better life for herself.

When young children dream about their future, it's usually about something they saw, heard, or experienced. How this is processed will most likely impact their lives forever. I developed a love for God at an early age. My mother started taking us to church when we were very young. We attended a church where having faith was the main focus. I remember when I was about four years old, and an evangelist walked up to my mother as I was standing with her. She said, "God has a great call on your daughter's life." I was not sure what she meant but I knew the word *great* was used, and even at the age of four, I knew *great* was a good thing. There may be negative things said to and about us, but there are also positive things said. I guess without realizing it, I received the positive things even then, which I believe has helped shape my life. I believe with God all things are possible.

Knowing oneself is not always easy. We are affected more than we realize by images of ourselves reflected by family, friends, and coworkers. We tend to go along with their assessments, without examining the very real possibility that they may be wrong. It is very important not to let other people's opinions stop you from doing *what you want*. According to Dr. Roy Menninger, "a most effective psychological tool for discovering what you really want out of life is the Goal Analysis." You do not need a psychologist for this. All you need are a couple of hours to yourself. The Goal Analysis consists of writing down the answers to the four questions that follow.

PERSONAL GOALS:

1. What do you want your personal life to be like a year from now? Grow spiritually, make new friends, change your appearance? Remodel your home, and become more independent? When you finish, you should have a detailed description of what you would like your life to be like in twelve months.

2. What do you want your life to be like in ten years? Where do you want to live? What kind of lifestyle do you want to have? Do you want to build your dream house? Write it all down. Paint a word picture of your life as you would like it to be in another ten years.

CAREER GOALS:

1. Where do you want to be in your business or professional life ten years from now? Be specific and realistic. What position do you want to hold? How much money do you want to be making? What organization or company do you want to be working for? Do you want your own business?

2. Where do you want to be in your business or professional life one year from now? Be even more specific here. Do you want a promotion? What kind? A new job? A raise? How much? Do you want to pursue a degree? Attend graduate school?

Put your analysis away in a safe place for two weeks, then set aside a couple of hours to go over it. You will probably want to make changes. Even if you have not given any thought to your analysis during these two weeks, your brain has been working away on it, assessing what you have written, and making additions and deletions. Freud called this process "the unconscious at work."

**DO NOT CONFINE YOURSELF
TO THESE FEW QUESTIONS;
THEY WERE JUST TO GET YOU THINKING.**

At the age of ten or eleven, I kept a diary. I would not just write things I did daily, I would also write about how I wanted my life to be. I set my dreams to paper. For example, I had this dream of graduating from high school, going to college, and becoming a teacher. I dreamed of getting married to my Mr. Wonderful, who would be spirit-filled because I wanted a peaceful home for my family. I wanted to have four children, two boys and then two girls, in that order. I lived in Chicago all of my life so I wanted to move to another state, where I would continue my education.

Yes, all my dreams came to life except one. I have not earned my doctorate degree—yet. No, things did not happen in the order I planned, and it was not a smooth journey.

MY DREAM JOURNEY BEGINS

This is how it went. I graduated in June 1977, and married September 1977. The plan was to start college the spring of 1978. When spring came, I was pregnant with my first child. I still attempted to start class, but had to withdraw because it was a difficult pregnancy.

I had to put school off for about fours years because the babies started coming every year. When my third child was a year old, I set out again to finish what I started. I started class the spring of 1981, taking night classes. Things were going fairly well but I got pregnant with my fourth child in May of 1981. I refused to let this disturb me at this point, because I knew *what I wanted*. Yes, I was pregnant, but I was determined to go back to college the fall of 1981.

Fall came and off to class I went. Near the end of the pregnancy, I started to have complications. My doctor had concerns, but I told him that I was so close to finishing the semester that I had to continue. He gave me instructions and I followed them to the letter. This was December and the baby was due in January. I did not know how I was going to make it, but, with the help of God and my husband, I made it.

The children were getting older and in school, so I put my formal education in the back of my mind, never letting the dream die. I gave all of my attention to my family. I loved teaching my children, and the special time we all had together. I volunteered at their schools. My oldest son had a learning disability, so I gave him a lot of attention, helping him in any way I could, working very closely with his teachers and the school. Making sure I took care of myself, I made an appointment for my annual physical to make sure I was in good health. I finished my check-up and the doctor told me that I was pregnant with baby number five. Good Lord! This was pretty traumatic for me. Remember, I planned to have only four children, two boys and two girls. I became a blubbering mess, crying hysterically. I got over it after a couple of days, and moved on with life.

We moved to Texas, where my husband was called to pastor, in June of 1988. This was a major challenge for our family. We had new adjustments and major challenges. My life was dedicated to taking care of my family, and helping my husband to build the ministry. I was busy and not sure of many things, but I trusted God and loving my family made life grand.

To be of some financial help, I provided care for a couple of children around the same age as my youngest son. This turned into a small business, as I provided licensed home daycare. I did this until my youngest was in kindergarten. Then, I went to work for a corporate childcare facility as the center director. This position required long hours, which interfered with me being home with my children after school. I eventually went to work at the elementary school my youngest child attended. This put me on the same schedule as the children. They loved it and so did I.

My husband came across some information on how I could earn a bachelor's degree while preserving my work schedule. Back to class I went in the spring of 1996. This worked out great. With the exception of the youngest, the children were in high school, and everyone helped out. I attended class two nights a week and some Saturday mornings. During this journey, I became torn in all directions. Our church opened a child care facility in which I was the director, my oldest son became chronically ill, and then there were all the teenage issues that required attention.

Through it all, I managed, with God sustaining me. I earned my bachelor's degree in Business Management in December of 1999.

The child care facility closed in August of 2003, and I started back to college to earn my master's degree in Rehabilitation Counseling. I decided on this major because I wanted to become more knowledgeable as to how I could help my son. During this time, I worked full-time at a major workers' compensation company as a records clerk. I left there to work at a rehabilitation medical center as a job-coach developer to assist disabled individuals become gainfully employed. My internship was with the Division for Blind Services, which was very enlightening. I am currently employed as a Vocational Rehabilitation Counselor and loving it. I have learned a lot that has been helpful to my son, but not enough. I am in search of better treatment for him and other individuals fighting the battle of mental illness.

I trust God in all things, and will continue to believe He will aid me in my search. Isaiah 40:31 says, "Yet those who wait for the Lord will gain new strength; they will mount up with wings like eagles, they will run and not get tired, they will walk and not become weary" (NASB). This scripture gives me daily strength, and hope for better treatment for individuals with severe mental illness, so they can go on to live successful lives.

This is what I want. And this is what I'm going to get—with God's help.

About the Author

Rochelle L. Owens, is a Vocational Rehabilitation Counselor for the state of Texas, a ministry speaker who believes that with God, all things are possible, and a Mary Kay beauty consultant. She provides a weekly motivational e-mail that encourages individuals and assures them that whatever they believe, they can achieve. She served for ten years as the youth leader at her church, and for five years as director for YW-Teens, a program providing leadership for girls ages ten through eighteen in the Richardson School District. She has earned a bachelor's degree in Business Management and a master's in Rehabilitation Counseling.

She has been happily married for twenty-nine years to Pastor John Owens II, and God has blessed them with five wonderful children, and eight adorable grandchildren. Her greatest accomplishment is taking care of her family. Rochelle's drive in life is to find the best treatment available to enable her oldest son, and others like him, to live successful lives. There has to be better treatment for individuals who are fighting the battle of mental illness. She resides in Addison, Texas, with her family.

Chapter 6

Possibility Thinking

BEVERLY GIPPLE

"Possibility thinking" is the practice of believing and behaving as though a goal or desire of your heart is possible, regardless of appearances or prevailing opinions. This is not a definition I found somewhere and adopted. Rather, it is the result of a natural progression of events, conversations, and observations I have experienced over my lifetime. Basically, I got it from Daddy and God.

From my father, a highly focused, compassionate, and intelligent man who absolutely shaped my life, I inherited and learned the belief that at least one more step toward a goal or dream is possible. He accepted and nurtured me as a child, and provided continual information and support while I was growing up. We shared unconditional love, humor, wisdom, and appreciation throughout our sixty-four years together. He was a remarkable man possessed of uncommon good sense. When he was in his mentoring mode, he would often look at me and say, "Now, remember this. **The difficult, we do immediately. The impossible takes a little longer**."

My birth and early years were a strong test of that belief in the impossible being possible. Those years also taught me the value of doing what was "doable," no matter how small a step it was. I was born with eight fingers and malformed feet that would not permit me to walk. I can only imagine the shock and grief my young parents experienced as they heard well-meaning family and friends say that it was a tragedy that their baby girl would probably never walk. No one had ever seen such bone formations, not even the doctors and specialists at the University of Iowa Children's Hospital in Iowa City, Iowa.

What people had not counted on was the strong, absolute belief my parents had in God's ability to make all things right. So we went to the doctors and began to do the impossible—build feet and legs for me so I could walk. I don't remember conversations, of course, but I do remember the feelings of deep, deep grief and pain my mother carried. In fact, she never fully released them, and she refused to talk about them. My father never talked about it either; he was too busy working on the problem to get stuck in his emotions.

The beauty of our situation was that God provided us with two exceptional doctors: Dr. Steindler, who eventually went on to write a basic textbook for surgeons, and Dr. Ponseti, a young Spanish doctor who had come from Mexico to intern with Dr. Steindler, and then spent his life researching feet malformations like mine. Dr. Ponseti told the receptionist at the hospital clinic, "The Gipple baby is mine. Take her out of the normal rotation." I like to think that the attachment formed between us and the success we achieved encouraged him to pursue his later research. When I went back and saw him in 1986, he greeted me like an old friend, showed me the improved facilities, and took great pride in the fact that I was still walking very well. The University Hospitals later opened the Ponseti Clinic for Club Feet. I now recognize that both of my doctors were also committed to finding solutions to impossible situations. Isn't it amazing and comforting to recognize how God brings to us souls who match our belief system?

I can imagine the "possibility thinking" conversations Daddy probably had with the doctors, because he always kept asking for information about the goal and was always searching for the next doable step. I'm sure that the conversation in 1940 at the Children's Hospital in Iowa City, Iowa went something like this:

> Doctor: Mr. Gipple, we have never seen anything like this. We don't know what to tell you.
>
> Daddy: Well, Doc, what do you see that can be improved?
>
> Doctor: Well, her toes are webbed. We can separate them.
>
> Daddy: OK. Let's start there.

And so they did. Over the six-year period of twenty-one surgeries—with wheel chairs, walking casts, and physical therapy—the doctors cut tendons, chipped away bone, rotated feet, fused ankle bones, and spliced heel cords. The result was that, slowly but definitely, these servants of God built me feet that would let me finally walk at age six. It's true that I walk differently from other people, but then I've noticed some other "funny walkers" also, so I'm okay with that. The best news of all is that, although the doctors predicted I would be in a wheelchair permanently by 1979, I am still walking under my own power.

The difficult we did immediately; the impossible took six years.

As a child, I thought that Daddy's motto just meant that he was a positive person, and it was a good goal—probably not attainable, but a good goal. However, as I became an adult, I realized that both my parents put our lives in God's hands every day with total trust, gratitude, and commitment. Daddy's motto was a natural outcome of my parents' beliefs and experiences. When you live on a farm, you realize that man is not in charge of things. Oh, we make decisions and plans, but over everything is God's plan for the land, the weather, the animals, the crops, and even you and me. Your job is to take care of things and maintain a quality of life that serves God. This awareness comes early and completely shapes your thinking and expectations. I remember Daddy telling me that if he prayed like everything depended on God and worked like everything depended on him, then things usually worked out for good.

Some people pray; others meditate. Daddy did all of that, but he also relied strongly on dialogue. When he needed an answer, he would tell God the question when he went to bed. Then he would wake up at 2:00 a.m., write down the answer and go back to sleep. Daddy never said when he started this pattern, but he often discussed how important it was to talk to God and expect an answer. I've not had success with the 2:00 a.m. strategy, but I do tell God what is on my mind and heart when I go to sleep, and then pay special attention to my thoughts as I come out of dreamtime the next morning. My answers usually come in the form of how to focus on the possible and look for that next step, no matter how small it is. While Daddy and Mother taught me to walk with God every moment of my life, to expect God to hear and answer me, and to live with joy and gratitude, they also taught me to focus on what was right and good about my life and to use the gifts I have to achieve whatever I wanted.

I remember crying in the kitchen one summer day because Mother could not find a piano teacher for me since I only had eight fingers. Daddy had come in from the field to get a drink of water and asked what was wrong, so I told him. He thought for a while.

Daddy: Is playing the piano very important to you?

Me: Yes! Everybody in our family plays the piano and I want to, too.

Daddy: (after thinking a while) Can you read music?

Me: Yes. (I had started trumpet lessons)

Daddy: Do we have any piano lesson books in this house?

Me: Yes. (Our music cabinet was full of books from Daddy, Mother, and my brother.)

Daddy: Can you think of anyone who can help you if you get stuck?

Me: Yes. (There was that incredible possibility thinking again!)

Daddy: Well, maybe your problem is not as big as you think it is.

He finished drinking the glass of water, went back outdoors to the tractor, and drove off down the field. I hurried to the music cabinet, dug out the lesson books, and eventually taught myself to play the piano well enough to play for church. My impossible situation was no big deal in my father's perspective. That's how you handle situations that look like dead ends.

This philosophy that anything is possible has permeated every part of my life, especially my teaching and counseling strategies. When someone needs or wants change, I help him or her look calmly and clearly at the situation. I help them decide what it would take to get where they want to be, or at least to take that next step toward their goal or dream. I also help them recognize how much they can do themselves and how much someone else would need to do. Finally, I counsel them to go to that someone else to ask that person for assistance.

Over the years, I have found myself saying that there are really no dead ends; there are just problems we don't have answers to yet. Think of all the breakthroughs, even in just our lifetime, that occurred because someone refused to believe that something was impossible–a walk on the moon, the four-minute mile. These are examples of "possibility thinking." One of my heroes has always been Thomas Edison. Instead of saying that he had failed five hundred times while inventing the light bulb, he is reported to have said that he had found five hundred ways that were not the answer. Wow! What a shift in perspective! Richard Bandler and John Grinder, founders of Neuro Linguistic Programming, call this "reframing"(1982).

As I think about my experiences, I realize that there is a core of truths that can help all people live their dreams. These truths I've learned include: (1) Find and live your "heart song;" (2) Believe that all things are possible—even dreams; and (3) Get a trouble-shooting strategy that moves you toward those desires.

FIND AND LIVE YOUR "HEART SONG"

What is your passion? When do you feel really alive and happy to be participating? Singing and teaching are my "heart songs." I started teaching my dolls when I was three. The content and the students have changed over the years, but never my need to teach. When Johnny Wimbrey said that he was "called to serve," I said, "Me, too!" I serve by empowering others through information, support, and acceptance. It's always been easy for me to grasp concepts and then put them into either words or an example that helps others understand and use the information. Teaching is the perfect fit for me. I've held other jobs, but helping people find their own strength and walk forward with confidence is what makes my heart really soar and sing.

BELIEVE IT

Did you know the Universe is always striving to prove you right? I know many people feel that they battle the Universe. They believe that nothing ever goes right for them. But what if the problem is their own beliefs? What if they believed, even expected, things to be hard or go wrong, so that is the situation created—by them! Scary, isn't it? After much observation, I've realized that it's true for me. It's exciting to consciously observe my thoughts and then see how they relate to what happens in my world. Think about times when this was true for you, and then begin to live your life as though it truly were possible to do, or have, whatever you needed or wanted. **Possibility thinking** is at the core of this process of defining goals, deciding on strategies, and creating your life.

What impossible dream have you had for your life? Consider the possibility that God gave you that dream. If that could be true, then couldn't you also consider the possibility that He will help you achieve it? That this special talent or this driving need is a signal as to what you were meant to do? I've heard many people share their belief that they knew they were destined to sing, farm, build, fly airplanes, or teach. For those of you who say that you have no special talent or desire, I suggest you look more carefully at yourself. The ability to work with animals or people in stress, or to speak to people in a comforting manner are equally valuable abilities. I strongly encourage you to spend time honoring yourself for all the things that you just naturally do without thinking. I believe that one of God's gifts to us is to make our passion look and feel easy to us, so we would be sure to do it. The problem comes when we don't honor that passion.

DEVELOP CONSCIOUS STRATEGIES

As I examine my life, focus, words, and actions, I realize that although I teach many subjects, I am really teaching how to learn.

I took the strategies I saw Daddy using in his life as a farmer and real estate broker and applied them to my work. After an argument with a school psychologist one day, I found myself explaining to the principal that there are two kinds of thinkers: slot thinkers like the school psychologist, who clearly define what is "today," and possibility thinkers, like Edison, who work to move us closer to the possibilities of tomorrow. In reality, we need to be both a possibility thinker and a slot thinker. "Slot thinking" lets you see clearly while defining the true problem. Then "possibility thinking" enables you to move forward into your success.

LEARNER, NOT VICTIM

For many years, I saw things that happened to me from the viewpoint of a victim stuck in slot thinking, and I just fell apart when hurtful or stressful things happened. Then I moved to "survivor," and became committed to the idea of success against great odds. That sounded like a positive statement until I realized that along with success, I was also claiming "great odds." Now, I choose to view my life as a never-ending series of lessons in spiritual growth as I participate in creating my life. When striving to show compassion and unconditional love by giving up judgment and criticism, it helps to realize that all of us are a "work in progress." If I am to be a learner, and not a victim or survivor, then I must consciously choose to keep a joyful heart and a positive attitude, to expect God's awareness and response, and to give up the "victim" mentality. The choice to expect positive events and supportive cooperation from others is as essential as the decision to stop complaining or expecting troubles.

LOOK AT THINGS DIFFERENTLY

Years ago, I realized that if I don't like what I'm looking at, I can choose to look at it differently. So now I consider the possibility that my situation is a gift, instead of a problem.

For example, I was devastated this spring when I lost three very significant loved ones in the span of one month. First, the man who had been my loving partner for thirteen years died suddenly of liver cancer. One week later, I lost my best friend due to an allergic reaction to medication after elective surgery. She was truly my "sister from another mother." I was just starting to deal with my grief, when three weeks later, my mother was finally freed from her six-year struggle with Alzheimer's disease. Naturally, I was overwhelmed. People offered comfort and said they couldn't imagine having to deal with all that at once. They didn't know what to say. I told them that it was okay, because I didn't know what to say either. It seemed impossible to comprehend, much less deal with. Then, I did what everyone else does. I got out of bed, dressed, faced the day, and did what was doable. And life moved on. Soon, it was another day, another week, another month, and I was still living and growing.

The result of my dearest ones passing on is that my communication with God has become of a much higher quality. A sense of peace and comfort has been steady, as I slowly gain strength and clarity again. Some people have said it would be "impossible" to deal with so much stress and grief. When these thoughts come, I can hear Daddy's voice saying, "You can do anything you set your mind and heart to. **Just remember—The impossible takes a little longer.**"

About the Author

Refusing to be limited by physical challenges or the beliefs of others, Beverly Gipple has pursued all of her life interests by following her dreams, and singing her heart song. Infused with her parents' philosophy that she can achieve success in any endeavor, Beverly is an accomplished teacher, writer, musician, and actress. A passion for communication has led her to become a mentor, motivator, consultant, and learning coach, as she gives acceptance and support to others.

Beverly has spent more than twenty years in the classroom, in both regular and special education. Holding lifetime professional teaching certification from the State of Iowa, she has taught elementary through master's level classes. Many years were spent training special education teachers and administering summer school programs for learning-disabled students. Her doctoral studies focused on brain function—how the mind works independently, and in conjunction with emotions and the physical body.

Currently, Beverly works as a tutor, learning coach, and mentor, teaching all ages and all subjects, except higher math and advanced science. Her special strength is the ability to simplify the concepts and connect them to the listener's experience and knowledge base, thus making the task seem doable, whether she is working with the learner or the teacher. Her main focus combines "Possibility Thinking" with strategies and techniques for "Learning How to Learn."

An irrepressible sense of humor and a keen mind help keep Beverly's classes and workshops lively and informative. Students often comment that they didn't know learning could be so easy and so much fun. Beverly offers development programs for teachers, parents, and service groups, in addition to her motivational and inspirational presentations. She also creates workshops for groups wanting specific content and work skills, as well as uplifting.

Committed to seeing the humor in situations, and enjoying the many opportunities for self-expression, Beverly's main message is that life is a "gift," and we are all here to serve and to support each other. This means that we embrace life as it comes—with awareness, good humor, and a genuine commitment to living our possibilities.

Contact Information: Positively Golden, 18484 Preston Road., Suite 102 PMB109 Dallas, TX 75252-5474 www.beverlygipple.com and bev@beverlygipple.com

Chapter 7

Life B.E.G.I.N.s Today

ADRIEL JONES AND ERIC BRIAN ROBINSON

For so many of us today, life has ceased to exist as we once knew it. It is as if we went to sleep and woke up in the land of make-believe. Up is down, right is left, wrong is right, good is bad, black is white, and life is death. Our very existence seems not to warrant any fanfare or celebration. In fact, many of us are beginning to wonder if anyone would notice if we were to die. Yes, life as we know it has ceased to exist.

We find ourselves in this situation for various reasons. Our lives have been devastated by divorce or shattered by the death of a close friend. Many of us are unemployed, fighting cancer or some other sickness, raising our children alone, or even visiting loved ones in prison. Yes, life has ceased to exist.

Some are stuck in a dead-end job, regretting the decision not to finish college, wanting to go back to school, but never being able to afford to go back and one day leave that dead-end job. Others are stuck in dead-end relationships they can't seem to leave. Still others have lost their faith in God, their faith in others, and their faith in themselves. Yes, life has ceased.

If only we knew then what we know now. If only we could go back and change some of our choices. Unfortunately, we can't go back and start over.

However, we can start now and make a brand new end. Life as we once knew it may have ceased to exist, but it definitely has not ceased. There are still bills to be paid, children to be taken care of, and loved ones to look after. No, life has not ceased. It is far from being over. In fact, if we so choose, life can B.E.G.I.N. today.

You might have guessed by now that B.E.G.I.N. is an acronym. Just as there are five letters in the acronym B.E.G.I.N., there are five steps to beginning life anew today. Following these five steps will help heal the wounds of the past, provide optimism for current problems, and restore hope in the future.

The first step in the process might be the hardest: We must Believe. Many of us find ourselves in such a rut that we don't see any way out. We must believe that improvement is possible in spite of outward appearances. So many of us harbor no real hope that things will get better, and find ourselves praying each day that things won't get worse. We are so locked into our sorrow, our despair, our hopelessness, that if God Himself were to come down and speak to us in the midst of our situation, telling us that it will be okay, we would scarcely believe Him. But in order for life to B.E.G.I.N. today, we must believe.

Some of you, no doubt, are about to stop reading. You've given up on God long ago. You don't believe in Him or any other "higher power." You've accepted your current lot in life, and doubt that there is anything "better" out there for you. For those of you who accept this as truth, there is bad news: You are addicts. If you accept the idea that there is no God and that your problems cannot be solved, you are addicted to your problems; locked in to your situations. Why else would you not free yourself of such burdens?

The truth is, many of us often find ourselves in trying circumstances, not by anything God has done, but because of the choices we've made. Even now, the choice is ours. We may have given up on God, but He has never given up on us. No matter what you choose, the fact still remains that we must believe in something greater than ourselves.

We must believe that we can beat the cancer or other infirmity. We must believe that we can happily live our lives, although a loved one has passed away. We must believe that we will find a job. We must believe that we can raise our kids, even if we must do it alone. We must believe that our situation can, and will, be different. In order for life to B.E.G.I.N. today, we must believe.

> *The greatest discovery of any generation is that a human being can alter his life by altering his attitude.* —*William James*

The "E" in the acronym stands for "Establish control." Establishing control begins in our attitudes toward our lives. A proper attitude is the key to not only establishing control, but also to success. Establishing control requires us to take inventory of the things in our lives.

In everyone's life there are situations that can and cannot be controlled. Too often, we like to focus on the situations that we can't control, rather than on the ones we can. We become frustrated, depressed, and angry over things we can't control. We spend hours considering, reflecting, and pondering what would have been, could have been, or should have been. We have to stop wasting valuable time on the uncontrollable. Instead, we must establish control over the things that we are able to.

I was twenty-two years of age when I encountered a life-transforming event. It was one I was ill-equipped to handle, but still had to deal with despite my challenges. I had recently graduated from college when the mother of my children told me she no longer had the desire to play a part in the rearing of our two small children. To say the least, I was shocked! It was beyond my comprehension how this woman who had given birth to two beautiful babies could just walk out of their lives without any regard or regret. But she did. It was a situation I initially attempted to control through communication and mediation, but the more I attempted to control the situation, the more it seemed to worsen. I learned that you can't control the decisions of grown folks, no matter how hard you try. I realized that the only thing that I had total control of was my positive attitude in dealing with a negative situation.

Charles Swindoll said this about attitude:

> The longer I live, the more I realize the impact of attitude on life. Attitude, to me, is more important than facts. It is more important than the past, than education, than money, than circumstances, than failures, than successes, than what other people think or say or do. It is more important than appearance, giftedness, or skill. It will make or break a company . . . a church . . . a home. The remarkable thing is we have a choice every day regarding attitude we will embrace for that day. We cannot change our past . . . We cannot change the the fact that people will act in a certain way. We

cannot change the inevitable. The only thing we can do is play on the one string we have, and that is our attitude . . . I am convinced that life is 10 percent what happens to me and 90 percent how I react to it. And so it is with you . . . we are in charge of our attitudes.

It's not about what we can and cannot control, but how we deal with it. Once we have established control of our lives, we can begin to influence our homes, workplace, community, and the world in which we live.

Do whatever it takes, but don't take whatever. —Cheryl W. Robinson

The next step, "G," stands for "Get dirty," which is just a simple way of saying "do what needs to be done." However, do it without prostituting your character and integrity. Once you realize what you have to do, take control of the situation and don't hesitate to take action. If you have to try new things, then try new things. If you must come out of your comfort zone, then just do it. If you must sacrifice something now in order to have more later, then do it!

Make sure you understand what you want, why you want it, and what you're doing to get it. Don't compromise your character and integrity for money, fame, or power. People who selfishly fall into these traps usually inherit unexpected unhappiness.

Are we saying that money, fame, and power are evil? No. They have their place. They are tools for helping us obtain the things in life we desire. However, as desires themselves, they are nothing, even less than nothing. At best, mere distractions; at worst, addictions! When you need to get dirty to get the things you want, don't cheat yourself and don't compromise—not even once (regardless of the reason). So how can you keep from compromising yourself? Simply ask yourself, "How can I make money doing what I love to do?" The answer you give makes it progressively easier to continue down your road to success.

You might also ask, "How can I add value to people's lives while doing what it is I love?" Now, you're in a win-win situation. By adding a human factor, you get what you want, plus an added reward.

In the 1980s, Nike coined one of the most famous and easily recognized slogans in advertising history, "Just Do It." When this slogan came out, people were asking, "Just do what? What is "it"?" The 'it' in the slogan, of course, isn't referring to any one thing. That is because the "it" is up to you. Only you know what it is that you love. You have to go out there and do whatever it takes to get whatever it is you desire accomplished. You can't be afraid of getting dirty.

> *If you want to be truly successful, invest in yourself to get the nowl-edge you need to find your unique factor. When you find it and focus on it and persevere, your success will blossom.* —Sidney Madwed

"I" stands for Invest and Investigate. We invest in many things in our lives, but very rarely do we invest in anything worthwhile. Watching television, barhopping, and surfing the Internet are just a few examples of how we don't invest our time properly. We need to make it a priority to start investing in things that will better us as individuals. For example, if we want to go back to school but can't afford it, we should spend time educating ourselves on available financing. We should search for scholarships, grants, loans, or other ways to help us change our situation. Don't just talk about it, be about it.

You have to think in terms of investing for greater returns. Work, time, practice, effort, and sacrifice are just forms of investment. The more we invest, the greater the return will be. Always know that life is what we make it. If you want to win, you have to work like a winner. Very few receive the great returns, because only a few are willing to make the great investment.

Recently, I had the opportunity to join a nationally touring stage play that cast some notable stars in the entertainment industry. I invested a lot of hard work and time learning my lines and developing my role. I was excited because I would be living out a dream that my wife had rekindled through her encouragement. Although I had performed in college, church, and local productions, this was going to be my first major theatrical production.

Unfortunately, I allowed my excitement to overtake my sound judgment. I silenced the inner voice that was telling me, "Something is not right!" Suddenly, the opportunity fell from grace. The play was cancelled due to some questionable business practices. I had placed myself in a position where I was risking my reputation and my dream.

We must realize that not everyone has a caring or concerned attitude about our gifts, or our success. You have to be the best caretaker of both. Cherish your gifts as you would any treasure. Be sure not to entrust them to pirates! Be cautious with whom you share your dreams. You surely don't want them to turn into nightmares.

While my professional acting debut was not lived out through this venue, I've learned several valuable lessons. I guess the most important one is not to trade integrity for recognition. I am not going to delve into all that happened with this experience, but I will say "The Show" will go on! Based upon this life lesson, I've decided, along with the assistance of my wife, to write my own theatrical production. Look for it on Broadway!

Never, never, never give up! —Winston Churchill

Beginning life anew is not easy. That is why "N," the last step in the process, reminds us Never to give up. Giving up is easy. We will be tempted to quit, but we must resist that temptation and hold on. Life favors those who are able to stick with things when the going gets tough, because it does get tough at times. That is part of life's challenge.

Anyone can quit. In fact, most people do. If we choose to quit, we will have chosen to do nothing. If we choose to do nothing, our situation has no possible way of changing. As much as we want it to, or wish it to, our situation will not magically change for the better by itself. We must be active participants in helping guide our lives in the direction we desire. We must have the courage and strength to hang on and refuse to give up. This mindset will dramatically increase our chances of winning. If we sit and do nothing, we will have died, never having lived.

No matter the situation, life can B.E.G.I.N. today. We can B.E.G.I.N. today to Believe. We can B.E.G.I.N. today to Establish control. We can B.E.G.I.N. today to Get dirty. We can B.E.G.I.N. today to Invest in life and in ourselves. We can B.E.G.I.N. today to decide Never to give up. Be encouraged, have hope, for life B.E.G.I.N.s today.

About the Authors

Adriel Jones is a born teacher and speaker. His passion to help people is evident in every class he teaches, every speech he gives, and also in his first book, *A Guide to Parenting: Advice from a Guy with No Kids . . . Yet*. Possessing wisdom well beyond his years, Adriel has experienced many highs and lows in life. Proof positive—Jones earned a master's degree at the age of twenty-four; he also weathered a painful divorce. Nevertheless, he has never allowed adversity to dictate his life. His belief that life can begin anew each and every day rings through in every message he presents. To find out more about this inspiring young speaker, please visit: www. adrieljones.com.

Adriel Jones Enterprises
PO Box 330453
Fort Worth, Texas 76163 • 682-556-0585

Eric Brian Robinson is emerging as one of Dallas/Fort Worth's premier motivational speakers. Robinson is rapidly and innovatively charting a new course in the realm of personal growth and development. He uses a unique style of combining creative forms of communication to deliver his message. "I believe I bring a fresh approach that inspires the hearts and minds of people through skits, drama, and poetry," he said.

Born and raised in Buffalo, New York, Robinson had more than weather to contend with. Growing up in high-rise projects, a troubling family environment, disappointing academic challenges, and teen fatherhood (which eventually led to single parenting), presented Robinson with more than his fair share of obstacles. The Johnson C. Smith University graduate refused to allow the adversity he encountered to dictate his future. Instead, he built upon it! The psychology major is definitely shaking things up in the genre of motivational speaking. For more information, check out www.ericbrianrobinson.com.

Two the Top Enterprises
PO Box 182177
Arlington, Texas 76096 • 817-542-5015
1-(877)-ALWAYZE (259-2993)

Chapter 8

The Gift of True Purpose

CHRIS & JULIE CHOJNOWSKI

*Wrapped up in every experience in life, whether it be favorable or chal-
lenging, is a gift from God. It is our divine birthright to personally
develop ourselves to the fullest so we can know our truest purpose as an
expression of these gifts.*

What an amazing journey life is; a woven tapestry of every emotion
imaginable! And with each experience, we're given the opportunity
to grow and deepen our relationship with our creator, and with
ourselves. What we've come to realize, especially, through our relationship within the field of personal development, is that working
on ourselves has made all the difference in how we are able to move
through challenges, and also accelerate our experience into creating
more joy and harmony in our lives than we ever thought possible.

If you stand back and take a look at yourself and your life, wherever you may be at this moment, who and what do you see at first glance? Without any judgment upon yourself, ask: Am I already successful in all areas of my life? Am I finding happiness in my life on a continual basis, or am I someone who is unclear, or hesitant, about discovering the "true" meaning of what my life is all about? Am I living each day to the fullest, or do I think about past failures that no longer exist?

It is our experience that each and every one of us has amazing talents to bestow upon this earth. Moreover, we are here to give abundantly to everyone. As human beings, we naturally want to experience abundance all of the time. In fact, we look for it everywhere we go. In order for you to be optimally effective in your life, living a life that you love, and living a life with happiness, health, abundance, and enthusiasm, you *must* be in touch with your *true purpose* as a human being and be willing to *live into* a future that you create for yourself by inventing and reinventing your life on a continual basis.

So where do we start? How do we get there and how do we achieve success on a continual basis?

The answer is within our own thinking.

Rather than looking at yourself as someone who has had a series of things "happen" to you, make a decision today to look at your life as a series of moments just waiting for you to create into being. When you start *creating* your life this way, instead of looking outside of yourself for all the answers, then the chatter in your head about your judgments, and all the conversations you have about your past failings, begin to subside and eventually *disappear*. Then, and only then, can those negative thoughts be replaced by the forward movement of your own positive *thinking*. You are now free to be at *cause*.

We can gain this access to an empowering and purposeful experience in life through personal development education. By choosing to educate ourselves with personal development principles and practices, not only do we learn how to expand our view of ourselves and others, but we also learn how to make ourselves present with the all-important principles of universal law and integrity, which have been taught for thousands of years. We can learn how to become *unstoppable* in our lives, no matter what is happening, so we can move brilliantly onward toward what's next.

Your *true purpose* is connected to a creative way of *being in the present* rather than to something in the past, and through learning and practice, you will gain increasing clarity, and experience the exhilaration and joy of *every moment* as a result of your being open to the Universal Consciousness of God. Your life will no longer be about the past; it will be about whatever you want to *create now* and about a future that does not exist until you create it in the present. When you are committed to your purpose, you will begin to see that your life is a series of experiences that are continually moving you forward toward your goal, and that you can co-create your success with our creator. Because we are dealing with Universal Law, *we just can't lose if we choose to be connected to it. God wants us to keep moving forward, and will see to it that we do, no matter what.*

What we must simply learn is first to *align* our thinking with the Universal Laws and Success Principles that have existed for thousands of years. To validate this, ask a truly successful person how they got to where they are. Through careful observation, you'll find they either were aware of the very presence of the Universal Laws of Success, or their actions mirrored the principles of the Universal Laws, regardless of their inherent knowledge of them. Because human beings are not infallible, personal development is *essential* to success for everyone regardless of background. Because its benefits are so far reaching, personal development has proven itself time and again as something that is meant to be *running in the background* of our lives on a continual basis.

So if we have known about these Success Principles for thousands of years, why aren't more people living successful lives in all aspects? The truth is, most people never really get started. They never take that first step out of the box they have built around themselves as "protection" from "failure." If you want to get something different in your life, then you must create something *different* to cause this! If it feels uncomfortable in the beginning, then you're on the right track. Make a commitment toward what you *really* want to create in your life. You must generate a bold move. Begin it now!

Chris: One of our greatest breakthroughs came to us when Julie and I realized that we were going through our lives expecting success, without ever having written out a plan. We were continually challenged for forward movement in several areas of our lives. We then came across something in a Tony Robbins book called the "Rocking Chair Exercise." In this exercise, you imagine that you have reached old age, and are sitting on your porch in a rocking chair, looking back over the many years of your life. You are to imagine yourself thinking about the things you would not having accomplished in your lifetime. The exercise directs you to document every item you think about, and organize them into categories, such as financial, spiritual, and physical. We began to write down *every* single experience we desired to have in our lives before we pass on. We completed the list, knowing we would accomplish every single item we had written down. Within three years, *a door opened* that changed the course of our lives forever. We were clearly being led down a path leading straight to accomplishing *each specific goal* we had written down! This experience has lead the two of us to realize that our main purpose and essence as human beings on this earth is to further our own advancement, and to teach and give to others the same by simply being examples of that knowledge.

Let's shed some light on this a bit further. Life will give us just what we *think* about. This is called the "Law of Attraction." What you picture in your mind is what you are creating for yourself; what will manifest in your life. Take a good look and notice the thoughts you are thinking. Are you thinking thoughts about nothing, still trying to decide what to think? What is your result? Do you realize that everything surrounding you is a result of what you have thought about or pictured in your mind at some point earlier?

Know this: The creator is constantly preparing to give you whatever you choose, just by your thinking about it and then believing in it. So what do you desire? Know what you want, and be willing to take action to reveal the abundance God is giving you at this very moment. How truly powerful we are! We are born with the ability to empower ourselves by just thinking that we can accomplish something. Here's your opportunity to "*just do it*," because what you picture in your mind, you are actually manifesting into being!

Julie: Not only can we envision success for ourselves, but we can also envision success for *others*. We are continually surrounded by people who become instrumental to us throughout our lives.

One summer, when I was fifteen, I had the opportunity to join a gymnastics day camp with some former teammates of mine. It became one of my first-ever memorable breakthroughs in my life, as my enthusiastic coach made it very clear he had a vision for me to be successful. As we practiced throughout the day, I experienced a state of being where *I could never fail, no matter what*, as he spotted me through all the moves. He challenged me continuously by moving me ahead just enough, but not too much. He expected much of me, and taught me the importance of *momentum*—that as

I picked up both skill and speed, it would begin to move me along even further. The effect was amazing! I was able to learn new skills at a superior rate.

At the end of the summer season, awards were given as we spelled out C-A-M-P S-P-I-R-I-T. To my surprise, I was presented with one of my first awards ever, an "M" standing for "Mastery." It took me by surprise at first, as I hadn't fully grasped its relevance. As the years rolled on, the lesson has stayed with me. Because one person had a *vision* for my success and *acted* on it, it impacted my life dramatically. Because one person had a distinct vision for me to succeed above and beyond, I have been *empowered* to envision others to succeed greatly.

It is our birthright to live abundantly, and we can do this by learning how to generate and work with the "Law of All Sufficiency," which states that life is constantly giving us everything we need, and ushering us forward for personal growth and discovery. We must clear away any past thinking, or any thinking of lack, and replace it with a prosperity consciousness instead.

Again, our purpose in life is something we must *generate*. Once you are able to clear away your past, you can stand fully in the present. You are then left with, "Okay, what can I now create for my life and others?" Once you get this process started, then you will want to keep it moving forward because the effect you are creating is so exhilarating, and so fulfilling, there is nothing quite like it! You become unstoppable. When we learn how to open our awareness and learn how to apply success principles, we can generously move our lives forward as we teach this to others by example. What you will discover is that all that has happened to you in the past, whether favorable or not, *and* all that is happening to you now, is *continually moving you forward* so you can further your own self discovery.

It's not important whether you find things challenging or not. The fact is that once you realize this, you will be left with a completely new way of living your life. You are in the *flow* of God's Universal Consciousness, and you gain renewed confidence and meaning to now fully engage in it.

We are here to become aware that *all of life, and the experiences that come with it, are a gift, and that our truest purpose on this earth is to give this gift continually!* We must learn to continually grow and share it. Personal development education is one of the very best ways to accelerate and discover a renewed sense of purpose for yourself and others.

By learning to apply God's Universal Laws, and by *discovering our true purpose*, we can align with the most powerful way of being known to man in order to experience what is meant to be—abundant living to our absolute fullest expression.

About the Authors

Learn to master all areas of your life with a winning system for a lifetime of success! More information on how to apply the Universal Laws and Success Principles that Chris & Julie Chojnowski teach can be found at their websites: www.inspireintl.com and www.universallawsofsuccess.com.

For over a decade, Chris & Julie Chojnowski have been avid supporters of the Personal Development Industry, and have shared some very exciting opportunities to train and coach together. Chris has worked in the high tech industry for over fourteen years, and traveled worldwide for a Fortune 100 Company. Julie is a BDIC (Bachelor's Degree with Individual Concentration) graduate and holds a BA degree in Promotional Design from the University of Massachusetts at Amherst, and has participated within the Network Marketing industry for over the past fifteen years. She also holds a certification in Network Marketing, and has traveled extensively with other industry professionals, founders, and top income earners in the field. They are both currently involved as Founding Members and Field Advisory Board

Multiple Streams of Inspiration

Members with Success University of Dallas, Texas and together they are growing one of the largest and most successful Internet-based marketing teams with the company. They reside in the Boston, Massachusetts, area with their beautiful four-year-old daughter, Crystal Grace. They can be contacted via e-mail at cjc@inspireintl.com.

Chapter 9

From Goal Minds to Gold Mines

JOEL & KATHY DAVISSON

Start where you are with what you have knowing that what you have is plenty enough. —*Booker T. Washington*

The origin of all successful people, no matter how intelligent or successful they may be, is with an idea. The first thing you must do to begin on the road to success, is to think. What do successful people think about? They think about wealth, increase, success, and winning. What are the thoughts of unsuccessful people? They think about lack, poverty, doom, hopelessness, uncertainty, and impossibilities.

Jake Simmons, Texas millionaire and oil industrialist, said, "One-tenth of the folks run the world. One-tenth watch them run it, and the other 80 percent don't know what's going on."

In order to achieve success, you must start with a goal. Use all of the natural resources you have been given, and know that you were born to succeed.

Make It Your Goal to Find a Goal

Goals must first of all be believable; you attack the mental attitude first, then the physical attitude. Do you believe yourself worthy of success? Goals must be achievable, conceivable, and measurable. What gets measured, gets done. If you would write down twenty items, twenty things that you want to have, do, or become, you could accomplish the majority of them in five years and all of them within ten years. It's your time now.

The average individual gets four ideas a year, any one of which could lead to financial independence. Why won't they chase them? I'll tell you why. It's because they have been influenced by "stinking thinking." In the meantime, the Creator is knocking on your conscience, asking you, "Do you want more out of life?" The Creator will give you as much as you can imagine. What do you think of your chances of success?

The Universe Is God's Gold Mine

Before creating the universe, God had to think. In creating the earth he provided everything we needed to succeed in life. From the beginning of creation, God provided: 1) Light; 2) Water; 3) Air; 4) Fire; and 5) Earth.

As important as these elements are physically, they are important symbolically as well. Light illuminates, allowing us to see. To succeed we must have a vision. Water cleanses and quenches thirst. Similarly, we often must satisfy the needs of others in order to prosper. Just as air is necessary for life, you must surround yourself with people who will allow you to grow. Fire represents inspiration and motivation. The earth is where we work the soil to allow the success to grow.

Entrepreneur—To Enterprise
One Who Organizes a Business

The universe has four kingdoms—mineral, animal, plant, and human.

The lowest kingdom is the mineral kingdom, but it also is the richest. Minerals include gold, diamonds, and coal. Similarly, the mineral kingdom is important because it includes the soil necessary to nurture plants. The mineral kingdom absorbs the fossils of fish, fowl, and all living things, and provides a source of fertilizer for the plants to live. It gives of itself in order for the plant kingdom to succeed.

The plant kingdom is important because it provides vegetation, and supplies us with oxygen to breathe. The plant kingdom has to give of itself to fulfill the purpose of feeding animals and humans. Although animals live by eating plants, the animal kingdom has to give of itself to provide food and clothing for humans. Even if you are a vegetarian, you probably use leather goods. Everything has been given up for you to achieve success. The earth has provided us with the resources, and God has placed us here for a purpose. It is up to you to decide what you want out of life.

Think Yourself Clear—Do You Think
You Are Worthy of Success?

Psychologists report that the average person thinks thirty thousand thoughts per day. What you think about the longest will become the strongest. If people think positive thoughts most of the time, those thoughts will have a positive effect on their lives. By contrast, if people think negative thoughts most of the time, those thoughts will have a negative impact on their lives.

What you focus on the most will become a factor. If you don't control your thoughts, your thoughts will take control of you. Why does one individual see a half-glass of water as half full while another sees the same glass as half empty? One individual sees himself as being broke, and another sees himself as temporarily out of cash. In other words, get rid of your "stinking thinking." Some people are so negative; if you put them in a darkroom, they will develop.

The way you think—positive or negative—will have a direct influence on your level of performance, or potential. One of the first things you should do when you wake up every morning is take a moment to relax and mentally prepare for your day. Second, you should get prepared for the work of the day with a plan, or by organizing your list of priorities. Then, focus on everything that has to be done that day with a positive attitude, and do what needs to be done one thing at a time. Keep a positive mental attitude towards your goal.

Goals Are First Organized in the Mind

Goals must be realistic, and you will have to believe that you can achieve them. As you set your goals, ask yourself whether you believe yourself worthy of success. Ask yourself why some men succeed while others fail. Also ask yourself what constitutes success in life, and how you'll attain it.

The responsibility of success begins when you give yourself a pattern, a blueprint by which you can take possession of your own mind and put it into operation. All you have to do is follow the blueprint. Nothing within the realm of what is possible can withstand the man or woman who is intelligently bent on success. Every person carries within themselves the key that unlocks either the door of success or the door of failure.

Every year, many people choose to begin the year with a New Years' vow or resolution. Over and over again, they plan to lose weight, stop smoking, or to exercise more. Many of these vows, of course, are never achieved. In order to be successful, the first thing to do is make up your mind not to be set up for failure. Quit starting over, and finish what you have started. Begin to end failure. Pick up where you have left off and make that be your goal. Success will have a direct influence on your level of performance, or potential.

You Were Born to Win—Success Is a Birthright

Every person is equipped as only God can equip them. What a fortune we possess in our marvelous body and mind. In the realm of the mind, man is limitless in character. Likewise, there are no limitations on spirit, save those which we impose upon ourselves. When one is awakened to a sense of his limitless possibilities, he needs to know and understand the universal laws for growth and development. Only after you get a glimpse of yourself as your Maker intended you to be, only after you see yourself as successful, is it possible for you to be successful. Nothing and no one but yourself can prevent you from attaining your ambition.

You were born to win. Perhaps you didn't realize it the first moment you took a breath, and maybe it never occurred to you later. Yet it is an unmistakable fact that you were born to win. Your birthday is worth celebrating. All people are born with an innate capacity and ability, and given the opportunity and time, could become philosophers, poets, artists, and musicians. All people are born with the potential to become great, a hero, president. All that is needed is the opportunity and the time for development. It is within every person to be somebody, or to do something worthwhile in the world. The man who does not do it is violating his sacred birthright. The truest way to aid the body, and the surest method by which abnormal physical or moral conditions can be overcome, is through mental development. By getting the mind right, you can create the right atmosphere, and enlarge your horizons. In the words of Les Brown, "Shoot for the moon. If you miss, you will still end up in the stars."

Success Is Believing in Yourself

We were born and made to express happiness, gratitude, and joy. We need to realize that we do not need to look outside of ourselves for what we need. The truth is we are our own greatest asset, if only we can believe in ourselves. In other words, we need to obey the laws of attraction and keep our minds positive, so that we will attract abundance toward our lives. Prosperity and abundance follow a law as strict as that of mathematics. If we obey it, we get the flow; if we strangle it, we cut it off. The trouble is not in the supply; there is an abundance awaiting everyone on the globe.

The majority of us still believe in the idea of competition. Remember, you were born to win, and must march to the beat of a different drummer. You must believe in yourself, as Steven Corey says, "When no one else does." When we realize that we do not need to look outside ourselves for what we need, that the source of all supply, the divine spring which can quench our thirst, is within ourselves, then we shall not want. There is no law by which you can achieve success in anything without expecting it, demanding it, and assuming it. There must be a strong, firm self-faith first, or success will never come. There is no room for chance in God's system and supreme order. Everything must have a cause—a cause as large as the result. A stream cannot rise higher than its source. A fish cannot swim without water. A bird cannot fly without feathers.

Great success must have a great source, great confidence, and great expectation. Moreover, one must be persistent and resilient to attain it. No matter how great the ability, how large the genius, or how splendid the education, your achievement will never rise higher than your confidence. He who thinks he can, can. He who thinks he can't, can't. This is an indisputable law. It does not matter what other people think of you, your plans, or your aims. Whether others call you a visionary, a crank, or a dreamer, you must believe in yourself. Remember, you were born to win, and as Dennis Kimbro says, "Success is nothing more than a statistical event."

Successful Achievement

The trouble with most people is they fail to focus on their abundance and success. Remember, the creator has given us everything we need to achieve success. We also must have the faith to achieve greatness. Finally, we get out of life what we concentrate upon. What we do, our environment, our position, and our condition, are the results of our focus and concentration. If we concentrate upon poverty, then we attract a flow of poverty, and have pinched our inflow of prosperity. If we believe we are unworthy and our conviction is that the best things in life are not intended for us, of course we shall get what we have concentrated upon. If, on the other hand, we have centered our thoughts along the lines of prosperity, of abundance, if we have believed that the best things in the world are for us because we are children of God, and that health, happiness, and prosperity are our birthright, and if we have done our best to realize our ideas, then we will attract abundance and success. As Zig Ziglar said, "If you know what you want to do, have, and become, you will achieve success. I'll see you at the top." I will leave you with this thought: Expect good things to happen and good things will begin to happen in your life. So the truth is that success is no secret. It's inside of YOU.

About the Author

Robert Lemon is an award winning national speaker, successful entrepreneur, author, and film producer. His film *Vision to Victory Field of Dreams*, a unique opportunity to show Robert's mentoring efforts in his community with urban city prodigies Santana Moss and Duane Starks, who dreamed and succeeded in going to the NFL, premiered at the 2006 Independent Black Film Festival.

Named a man of prominence, power, and prestige, Robert is a speaker who teaches others to take responsibility for their lives. As a leading corporate and college speaker, Robert possesses the ability to combine the ageless tool of storytelling, with a profound understanding of today's culture and highest ideas. With a keen sense of humor and heart-warming charm, Robert seems to effortlessly elevate and energize his audiences to pursue their dreams.

For years, thousands of people have been touched by his seminars. In addition, he has touched audiences in his extensive travels, including a trip to Cape Town, South Africa. Robert's profound presentations draw from his academic and professional achievements, from the US Air Force, corporate experience from the US Postal service, and as the CEO of Believe Your Dreams Inc. Robert's seminars about maximizing potential adds tremendous testimonial to the validity of his message.

Member of National Speakers Association

For more information, contact Robert at 1-877-621-1315
info@robertlemon.org
P.O. Box 171802
Miami, FL 33017

Chapter 10

Faith in the Future

JOBY WEEKS

Great people talk about ideas; Average people talk about things;
Small people talk about each other. —Anonymous

I'm looking at a poster on the wall in my office that says, "Which box are you looking outside of?" As I recollect these past couple of years, I can see in myself, my thoughts, actions, and programs that I was in one box that was inside another box inside yet another box inside an even bigger box.

I wonder which one I'm thinking in right now.

It's uncomfortable to be different, to actually think rather than just react. Stop now, and think about yourself. We like to think of ourselves as independent and free, right? So, where are you in your walk, your journey? Which box are you thinking outside of?

From the outset, I should tell you that nothing in this chapter is new. I'm sharing with you age-old principles of success that have worked for me and countless others who *apply* the knowledge in their lives and break free from the bondage so many others find themselves in.

To begin with, successful people tend to have faith that the future holds great things for them. As John Maxwell put it, "Where there is no hope in the future, there is no power in the present."

It can be difficult to have faith in the future when the present is shackles and broken dreams. However, difficult is not impossible. Consider the following fable.

In the United States of America lies a large industrial city which is the site of one of the world's largest slave labor camps. Located in and around the center of this city are community settlements where the slaves live. Each morning, the slaves move herd-like from their quarters into the slave labor camps. Each one is at his or her station by 7:30 a.m. Here, they report to their master for the day's duties. And here they remain chained until 5:00 p.m. when they're released to go home.

The slaves have no choice as to how many hours they must labor. Sometimes they are required to work overtime until their master tells them they may leave and go home. Each year, the slaves are told when to take their vacations, for how long, and when they must return. They have little choice as to how much money they earn as they are paid not what they are worth, but what the job is worth. They are allowed very little time for lunch and coffee breaks during the labor hours.

The slaves will remain in their chains in great fear because the master can punish them with the "firing" or "layoff" whip. Even some of the older slaves who have been good and faithful have felt the sting of the whip.

Day by day, year by year, the slaves toil and grow older, until the master decides it is time to release them to the retirement camps, where they're forced to sit idle and wait for death. Old slaves who try to keep working are sometimes whipped with a "stop-their-pension" whip.

I know these slave camps exist, for I once was a slave.

But now I am a free man who lives among the slaves. The reason I am free, is because I am in business for myself as a Network Marketer.

Yes, I am truly free. I arise in the morning as called for by my schedule. I decide my own hours. I even can sleep late while the slaves are at work. I haven't been stuck in traffic in years! I can vacation when, where, and for how long I please. I'm free to eat my lunch and dinner wherever and whenever I choose.

And of course, I can decide my own paycheck because I am not a slave. I can choose to work when and where I please and with whom I please. I'm free to stay in the city for as long as I want or to move on to greener pastures if I decide. I've seen many slaves sadly pack their belongings to leave their city in search of a new master, but it is always the same.

There is, however, a ray of hope for the slave. Slaves can buy their own freedom. The cost is not high, yet it seems high to those who do not have the courage to pay the price.

What is the price of freedom? ONE MUST BE WILLING TO BE ONE'S OWN MASTER. One problem: Things that are easy to do are also easy not to do!

As a matter of fact, it can be even easier not to do the easy things, especially when you are surrounded by people who urge the easy path, the safe play, the status quo. Our only defense is to choose our friends and associates wisely. As Mark Twain once said, "Keep away from people who belittle your ambitions. Small people always do that, but the really great make you feel that you, too, can become great."

Warning! It's the start that stops most people. Don't let the start stop you!

Are you ready?

You've heard it said before, success is a journey, not a destination. For me it's had its ups and downs.

For most of us, success would include good health, energy and enthusiasm for life, fulfilling relationships, creative freedom, emotional and psychological stability, and a sense of well-being and peace of mind.

It is said that being broke is a temporary situation, but being poor is a state of mind. The wealthy focus on what they want. The poor focus on what they don't want. They both get it because what you focus on expands.

My father used to introduce me as his entrepreneur-philanthropist son. At the time, I had no idea what that meant. I now realize he was conditioning me to become that which he saw in me. I am now blessed to give away more money a year than 90 percent of the world earns.

You see, there are certain laws in the universe. What goes up must come down. What goes out must come back. In reality, receiving is the same thing as giving, because giving and receiving are different aspects of the same flow of energy in the universe. You could call it the sowing and reaping process, or you might call it karma.

So, who am I? Who is Joby Weeks?

Well, I was born into a bloodline of nobility. Bloodlines are pretty important to some families. Prince Henry Sinclair, the Earl of the Orkney Islands, sailed to America and mapped it out from Nova Scotia to Massachusetts a hundred years before Columbus discovered the West Indies. (Columbus, as you may know, never set foot in what is now the modern-day United States.) The Sinclair were the Knights Templar who went to Roslyn in Scotland after the Crusades with a secret that various books and movies hypothesize about. William Sinclair built Roslyn Chapel and started the Scottish Rite of Freemasonry. In fact, the group's most valuable, oldest, and sacred relic is called the Sinclair Scroll at the lodge in Kirkwall. William was the first Grand Master of the Illuminated, or Enlightened ones in Scotland.

Both sides of my family came over to settle America on the *Mayflower* and were decorated soldiers in the American Revolution. I can trace my lineage to Charlemagne on my mother's side as well. My great-great grandfather, John Wingate Weeks, was Secretary of War under Presidents Harding and Coolidge, and on the monetary commission which hoodwinked congress into granting the power to coin and print money to a private banking cartel called the Federal Reserve System, which is no more federal than Federal Express! This was the perfect merger of power between the Corporation and State. That's the definition of fascism, and it happened right here in America!

Wingate's son, Sinclair Weeks, was Secretary of Commerce under President Eisenhower, who was in charge of getting the biggest loan in the history of our country from this banking cartel to build the Interstate highway system. My grandfather was on the board of directors of some major companies in the United States and was the president of Reed and Barton Silver for a while. These were enlightened gentlemen who believed it was important to send their kids to the Ivy League schools (especially Harvard and Yale) to learn to be The Masters, while the rest of society sent their kids to the public schools to learn how to work for The Masters.

Why do I tell you all this? Well, my dad and his brothers and sister grew up with everything they could ever want. His form of rebellion was attending Dartmouth rather than Harvard. Instead of taking over the companies our family controls, he decided to go to Colorado as a ski bum, and then became a Christian school teacher, not making more than $20,000 a year.

My upbringing was a little different. I had the blood in my veins and desire in my heart not to settle for a life of poverty. (It's hard living on less than $20,000 a month, let alone a year!)

So, I decided I was going to be a hustler for cash. I had to do it on my own.

I did whatever I could to make money. I wasn't fond of clothes from the Salvation Army and Good will. I wanted the new clothes, sneakers, and so on.

At the time, making money meant purchasing candy bars cheap from a discount wholesaler, along with magazines, and then selling them door-to-door. Because my father was an economics teacher, he was a key player in my developing entrepreneurial spirit.

Dad taught me that profits are better than wages. I learned to trade—especially to trade up.

In addition to trading the usual baseball cards and comic books, I guess I had an aptitude for business well beyond my age. When I was fourteen, I bought a guitar for $25, traded it for a $250 car stereo system, sold that for $300 and bought a home theater system—which I sold for $1,000. My uncle took the $1,000 and gifted me with a $5,000 Pioneer Elite 60-inch big-screen television. I sold the TV for $3,000, and bought some stock at 98¢ a share. I later sold a bunch of it at $14 a share, making around $40,000 by the time I turned fifteen. I then put $10,000 into a stock that was trading at 2¢ a share. It had jumped to $1.49 a share when I sold most of it! The money hasn't stopped replenishing itself and is still growing to this day. That's much more fun than actually working for money!

If I could do it again, I would have put a lot more cash in the stock, but instead of investing, I chose to buy a Ferrari 355 Spyder on eBay. An expensive doodad! That car in reality cost me $10 million! Why? Well, the money I could have made in the stock, I put in a depreciating asset because I acted on my emotions rather than my intellect. It taught me a valuable lesson. Maybe you can learn from my mistake as well. Instead of taking, let's say, $50,000 and buying the Benz, take the $50,000 and put it in an investment that pays you $1,000 a month. Five years later, the Benz is paid off, and you still have your $50,000 paying you $1,000 a month to buy another car.

Before learning about stocks and business, I thought that the best profit margins were in being a "street pharmacist." I was in network marketing and I didn't even know it.

I decided to make a change in my life after seeing friends go to jail, some even dying. I realized I could die, too. I had guns stuck to my head, screwdrivers held to my throat, and deals busted up for international drug smuggling. I drove a stolen car off a cliff, and even overdosed, ending up in the hospital on life support, all before I turned eighteen.

I found myself far from the Ivy League, blue-blood expectation my family had of me and was almost disowned. I just wanted to give up. After a lot of soul searching and prayer, The Creator brought to me a purpose for my life that I could fulfill with the *legal* Network Marketing business model, a proprietary patented product perfectly positioned in front of the next trillion dollar trend to hit the world—Wellness!

People are tired of sickness! They don't want to keep taking the deadly, debilitating, destructive, addictive, toxic pharmaceutical drugs that just treat symptoms and don't fix the cause of their health challenges. They are starting to take responsibility for their own health, and are searching for products with validated science that work. Educating people how to stay healthy or eliminate symptoms of disease will eventually make billions of dollars for the companies I oversee.

Of course, perhaps the biggest gift the Creator gave me was the gift of vision, the ability to see the opportunity before me. As Helen Keller famously said, "The only thing worse than being blind is having sight but no vision." Vision, however, is only part of the equation.

Vision without action is merely a dream.

Action without vision just passes the time.

Vision with action can change the world.

It's only when you clearly identify your purpose and set specific goals that you can fully unleash your God-given potential (and perhaps, undeveloped talents), empowering you to turn your dreams into reality. As soon as you know your "why," the "how" will practically take care of itself. It is a simple fact that, without a clear "why," a person tends to remain passive. When someone is passive, something terrible happens: nothing! To not make a decision is itself a decision, as Leo Shreven says. The neutral zone is not an option that successful people consider. You must be proactive, not reactive.

Deepak Chopra talks about the Wisdom of Uncertainty. The only thing that you know for sure is in the past, and if you are living in the past, your life will not be all that fun.

You always miss 100 percent of the shots you don't take. So I decided I was going to take my shot! I decided to defer college for a year and run with my entrepreneurial spirit; I found a mentor, was coachable, and built a business. I knew that if I worked a regular job, I wouldn't be able to sell it five to ten years down the road and that if I quit, I wouldn't get paid. I thought, "Hey, I'm going to put the time in anyway, so why not build an asset, something that will pay me while I'm sleeping!"

My family freaked, to say the least.

I was to become the first in a very long line to ditch college and get my MBA (Massive Bank Account) the nontraditional way. I began with the ending in mind. I knew what I wanted.

Here are some insights that might help you on your journey, as they have mine:

Truth #1: Problem-fixers make a lot more money than problem creators. Fix other people's problems and you will never have to worry about money again.

The easiest way to get what you want is to help others get what they want. It's always best if you are the only person who can provide them what they want. Those are the businesses and products I look for. Find something unique.

DO NOT be like most people—if you do, you will get what most people get, which is not much. Find a mentor and do what that person says; be coachable.

Truth #2: Bob Proctor told me, "Joby, do nothing yourself that you can pay someone else to do." I can mow my lawn; it would take an hour. I can also do what I do best and make, for the sake of argument, $100 in that hour instead and pay the kid down the street $10 to mow my lawn, earning me a $90 profit. **Learn about leverage**. Why get paid for eight hours a day, when you could get paid for 5,000 hours a day? If you build a network of 2,500 who work just two hours a day, you get paid on 5,000 hours a day! To get paid working yourself for 5,000 hours, you would have to put in 8 hours a day for 625 days straight with no breaks.

Truth #3: One thing we should never waste is time. The rich are not miserly; I've blown tons of money on trivial things. You no doubt have, too. Ever spend a week on the beach in a $2,000 a night hotel drinking $3,000 worth of champagne in a couple of hours? I know I have. If you haven't, it's something you gotta do at least once!

Stingy people have one thing in common; they are not truly rich, because they are not truly free. They play *not* to lose, rather than to win. Money doesn't buy happiness, as most would say. But money does buy you time. Time buys you freedom, and freedom buys you happiness. The truly rich do not waste their time doing that which returns very little.

Realizing this truth, I decided to cut out everything in my life that was not getting me closer to the life I envisioned for myself, the life I created in my mind. I had to change. I decided to enlighten myself. I looked at the year ahead and pretended it was the last year of my life.

If you were to die 365 days from now, what would you do in the meantime? Sit on the couch with a beer watching the TV? Or would you do something outrageous? Would you waste any time? I know I wouldn't.

So, every year I make a list of things I would like to do before I die. Then I go and do them. I try to out-do myself every year just for the fun of it. You will be surprised how much you can accomplish and how often you have to revisit your goals because you keep checking them off your list.

Truth # 4: Don't be afraid of change. I had to conquer my old habits and create new ones. I had to close off all possible avenues of retreat. The truly successful and the truly desperate have one thing in common: They are capable of anything. I was about to make a radical, life-altering decision.

I was finished playing games. My life was falling apart; watching my mother cry had some major implications, and gave me motivation to change. Not only was I hurting myself, I was hurting those around me.

Basically, there are two ways to change. Either you unlearn your present behavior, your habits, or you learn some new behavior to replace the old. I decided that it would be easier to learn new habits. Can you imagine trying to unlearn how to snowboard or ride a bike once you've mastered it?

First, I had to decide what I wanted my life to look like. I needed a map. A native in his home city always gets to the place he is going faster than a tourist, because he knows where he is going. You can go from Denver to Los Angeles a hundred different ways. You can skateboard, ride a bike, drive, walk, or take a plane. You can go directly or via Seattle. The possibilities are endless.

Likewise, you can become financially free a hundred different ways, though, of course, you must have a firm destination in mind and choose the appropriate vehicle to get you there. If you want to go to the moon, it doesn't matter what car you want to drive. A car is the wrong vehicle and won't get you there. You need a spaceship. You need to know where you are and where it is you want to be, and then chose the vehicle that will get you there the fastest.

I also had to decide what behaviors would express the outcome of my "dream" life.

In addition, I had to consciously embrace my new behavior. Every decision I made required me to first analyze, and then deliberately choose my new behavior. Split-second choices are what make up our lives. What you choose to do is determined by how you choose to feel. Of course, how you choose to feel is a direct consequence of how you choose to interpret each event in your life. If we choose a different interpretation or feeling, we will then take a different course of action. It's not the situation we find ourselves in, it's how we choose to react to the situation. With all the choices available to us, we have plenty of opportunity to take control of our lives.

One thing I found helpful was to practice my new conscious behavior until it became an unconscious behavior. It was hard at first. eric Hoffer said: "In times of change, learners inherit the earth, while the learned find themselves beautifully equipped to work in a world that no longer exists." So, I decided that learning should not end after high school.

Tony Robbins told me, "Joby, the only thing worse than not reading fifteen minutes a day is not thinking that it matters!" So, I have been reading at least two books a month for the last six years. Can you imagine how much more enlightened I am compared to my classmates, who graduated and haven't touched a book since? If you *can* read and you don't, you have no advantage over someone who can't read at all. As a matter of fact, I've given myself an education more valuable than any college could give me just by driving in the car listening to empowering CDs. That might be a clue as to why I control companies that make more money in a month than 90 percent of Americans make in a year. The fact that you are reading this now shows me you don't want to be a mind-controlled slave.

I've discovered that life is a process of self-discovery, bringing with it endless opportunities for change and growth. It follows that self-fulfillment involves embracing the changes that self-discovery brings. The key is to stay focused and ready for those opportunities to present themselves, as they always do.

Success, in some ways, is simply having the eyes to see, the courage to act, and the steadfastness to stick to it until the end. The quitters never win and the winners never quit. It's been said that dogs like bones. Actually, dogs like meat. They settle for bones. What are we settling for? Most of humanity is tiptoeing through life to arrive safely at death, finding the reasons and excuses to justify mediocrity.

This isn't a trial run! This is it! "We were not born winners, or losers; we were born choosers," says Anthony Clark. You have the choice to change, but how and why?

What if you knew it was absolutely impossible for you to fail in your business enterprise? What is it that would make your life worthwhile, meaningful and exciting?

Answer these questions:

1. How will my life be different once I am earning $500 to $1000 a month?

2. How will my life be different once I am earning $3000 to $5000 a month?

3. How will my life be different once I am earning in excess of $10,000 a month?

4. What would my life look like if my annual income suddenly became my monthly income, and I had the time to enjoy it?

5. What is the only thing that could cause me to give up and quit?

What we're talking about here is no less than fundamental change. As we know, change can be scary and difficult. However, change is what helps make life exciting. And without excitement, life can be empty. As Helen Keller once said, "Life is either a daring adventure or nothing."

Are you playing life not to lose or are you playing to win?

My father always told me: "The stupid person never learns from his mistakes. The smart person learns from his mistakes. The wise person learns from the mistakes of others. He doesn't have to touch the stove to know it's hot." If you are wise, you will only make promises you know you can keep. Promises to yourself are the most important; you must keep them at any cost. We need to promise ourselves that we are going to be authentic.

Authenticity is the harmony between who you are and what you do. It's the consistency between being and doing, between your essence and the life you lead. It's when what you do flows naturally from who you are. You can only act authentically if you know who you are. You know it instinctively. You also know who you are not. Think of the times you have felt that you were not being you. I can recall living my life as a rebel, knowing deep down, this is not me, this is not who I am.

Imagine the difference from the life you are living now, to the life you dream of. Imagine what it would be like to feel, with absolute clarity and conviction, that what you are doing is what you do best; that what you produce comes naturally from your essence. Imagine the feeling of effortless performance, of knowing that what you do is right because it feels right, it fits you perfectly, it suits you and is you. Successful people "make it look so easy" because being themselves is easy. For me, my life has become my business, and my business is my life.

Most of my friends are frustrated with where they are today and where their lives are heading. Frustration comes from a lot of effort producing little results. So the question is: What is it that I can do that requires the least effort for the greatest return? Well, logically, what is easiest is what comes naturally, automatically, from your true self. Most people go through life not knowing who they are or what they want.

I make money because what I do to make that money is authentically connected to who I am. In other words, I act authentically because what I do is what I do best. That's a big clue to getting rich. Do what you do best. In other words, be yourself.

The ego is your self-image. It is your social mask, the role you are playing. The ego thrives on approval. It wants to control and it is sustained by power because it lives in fear. Of course, I'm working on mine all the time. I realized that attention to the ego consumes the greatest amount of energy and is really a waste. After all, we can't please everyone all the time.

Your true self, your spirit, your soul, is completely free of those things. It is immune to criticism, it is unfearful of any challenge, and it feels beneath no one. Yet, it is humble, and feels superior to no one as well because it recognizes that everyone else is connected in spirit, expressing itself in different disguises.

No amount of money or success will solve the basic problems of existence. Only if you are intimate with yourself can you enjoy true happiness.

A lot of people "wear" what I call money repellent. They are not on the electromagnetic vibrational frequency that attracts money to them. They actually subconsciously repel money and opportunities away from themselves. You've seen people self-sabotage all the time. I speak all over the world to audiences mainly about how to position yourself for prosperity. I don't just teach it, I live it. Yet there are people who come to hear me speak, and walk out without taking action. Five years later, they are in the same spot, waiting for their break to come. They wouldn't see an opportunity if it slapped them upside the head.

When you admit that you are the author of you own life, you will realize that you have the power to change it. So, create the reality of your dreams today, and live with passion and purpose.

About the Author

Joby Weeks (better known as The Galavantor) is a modern-day Renaissance man. As a raver in his teens, he started out as a "street pharmacist," getting arrested for all sorts of things, going nowhere fast and stressing out his parents. He decided to make a change in his life after having guns stuck to his head, screwdrivers held to his throat, deals busted up for international drug smuggling, driving a stolen car off a cliff, and ending up in the hospital on life support as a result of an overdose. After a lot of soul-searching prayer, the Creator brought to him a purpose for his life that he could fulfill with the legal Network Marketing business model, a proprietary patented product perfectly positioned in front of the next trillion dollar trend to hit the world—wellness! Educating people how to stay healthy or eliminate symptoms of disease will eventually make the companies he oversees billions.

Now, at the age of twenty-four, he's spoken to audiences in all fifty states and over forty countries around the world on a whole array of subjects, empowering people to achieve freedom financially, spiritually, physically, mentally, and emotionally. He's been featured in numerous radio, newspaper, magazine and TV broadcasts worldwide, including T. D . Jakes' *Praise the Lord* Program on TBN.

Being single has given Joby quite a bit of freedom. Since 2002, he hasn't spent more than a week in any one place, which has given him the unique opportunity to network with some pretty powerful people around the world—becoming privy to deals most people don't even know exist.

He was the first teenager to reach the Top Position in a billion dollar Network Marketing Neutraceautical R&D Company and is now in the top one hundred money earners out of 1.2 million people.

He's been controlling the movement of millions of dollars since the age of twenty.

He oversees numerous international companies and loves to support various ministries.

He is the author of the highly anticipated book *Rich Mom Poor Dad* and *Secrets of a 20-Year-Old Millionaire*. He has sold tens of thousands of his CDs, *Secrets of a 20-Year-Old Millionaire* and *Interview with the Galavantor*. His *Freedom* DVD and e-book are also touching the world in a positive manner. Joby gives all the credit for his accomplishments to the Creator who put him in this time and place to accomplish His goals and plans through him. Joby says, "What the Creator can get through you, he will get to you."

When he's not climbing the tallest peaks in the world, jumping out of perfectly good airplanes, snowboarding in champagne powder, or scuba diving in the most beautiful reefs, Joby resides at his lakeside home in Denver, Colorado. Saying he is an avid adventurer is an understatement. His Web site is www.jobyweeks.com.

Chapter 11

Life Is About Choices;
Choose to Win!

PAUL BROWN

"Don't throw that away, son," my grandfather shouted at me from the other side of the old farm truck. "We can still eat that. Take that in the house and let Granny clean it up. It will make a nice dessert for tonight's meal." I picked up the carton of almost spoiled fruit along with the gallon of chocolate milk we had discovered and made my way to the house to give the food to Granny.

My grandfather was a pig farmer. He had made arrangements with local businesses and grocery stores to collect their rotten foods and table scraps, which he would use as food for his hogs.

Little did they know that my grandfather and I would sift through the musty lettuce boxes from the grocery stores and hot barrels of slop from the restaurants for our daily meals before we gave the rest to the hogs. I learned at an early age that life is all about choices. Choices are either good or bad, and rarely in-between. Some choices are made for us, but most of them we make ourselves. You can play the game of life to come out on top, or you can play just not to lose; I chose to win.

My name is Paul J. Brown, Jr., but you can call me Mr. Win Big. I'm a devout, born-again Christian from Haltom City, a small industrial town in Texas. If I could describe myself in one word, it would be "Visionary."

God gives me visions of goals, dreams, ambitions, and lifelong desires and helps me to see the big picture. Then, I do my best to bring the dream to life.

Someone once said, "Vision without action is a daydream. Action without vision is a nightmare." I believe that statement holds truth. You have to know where you are going in order to get there. Most people do not plan to fail, they simply fail to plan. Sometimes we allow other people to destroy our dreams because they fail to see the same visions and goals we do. They tell us every conceivable reason our dreams could go wrong, and convince us it would just be a waste of time to keep pursuing them. The key is never to let someone's mentality become your reality.

So many dreams are shattered before they've had a chance to shine because of the negative thinking of others. "You won't be able to start your own business because there is too much risk involved," we're told. Or a well-meaning friend might say, "My friend tried to start a business and it didn't work." Still others might say, "You will never finish college and find a good job because the market is too saturated."

Just because someone else's dream failed does not mean your dream will also. Society tries to place us all in groups or classifications based on what we can and cannot do, places we can and cannot go, and what we will and will not become.

With a childhood filled with memories of severe alcohol abuse, spousal abuse, domestic violence, and sub-poverty living, I was, by societal standards, a reject. Besides digging through slop barrels for my meals, I remember taking showers on the back porch with a water hose because the pipes had rotted under the house, which meant there was no water inside our home. I remember the constant eviction notices for nonpayment and countless nights in the dark because our electricity had been turned off.

When I was only sixteen years old, I watched my apartment burn down with everything I owned inside. From that point forward, I was separated from my family, and had to bounce back and forth from the homes of friends and extended family. I can even remember sleeping in my car many nights, just to have a place to lay my head.

According to the rules of society, I should have turned out to be a severe alcoholic, a terrible parent to my daughter, and an abusive husband. My life should have consisted of running from the law while living in a trailer park somewhere. But instead, at twenty-six, I am a very devoted father and husband, active in the church, and a well-to-do entrepreneur. I own numerous businesses, I make more money in a year than most lawyers and doctors, and I do not hold a college degree.

Society had its own set of choices and outcomes for me; I had a different agenda in mind because I knew what most people still haven't figured out: It's not what people call you that matters, it's what you answer to that counts!

Through all of my childhood mishaps and teenage troubles, I found something I was good at—football. I was ranked Top 25 in the state of Texas and Top 300 in the nation as a blue-chip player. I went on to play for a university in Oklahoma and we won the conference in 1999 and 2000. To this day, I still wear my huge conference championship ring on my finger as a reminder that dreams can come true.

I am currently a top-producing mortgage broker, million dollar-plus real estate agent, and real estate investor, among other things.

Just like many of you reading this book today, I was trapped in the corporate rat race. I was a leading sales rep for a major Fortune 500 company. I received numerous awards, including national recognition for being one of the top fifty sales reps in the nation for my company. I was promoted from sales rep to regional manager, and I managed more than twenty locations and over one hundred staff throughout the Texas and Oklahoma area. I went to all the corporate training and workshops, rubbed shoulders with the big wigs, and I just knew that one day I would retire rich and wealthy from this company and everything would be all right. Then one day, it finally hit me. I finally read between the lines and figured out what was really going on. I was building someone else's dream instead of building my own.

I decided enough was enough, so I started a small, part-time business offering financial services to lower- and middle-income families. I chose this market segment because of my background, and because that was where I derived my passion.

I soon realized I enjoyed building my business a lot more than I did building someone else's. With my corporate job, I was required to go in early and come home late, which did not leave much time for me to build my business or take care of my rapidly growing client base. My corporate job told me what I had to wear, when I could go on vacation, how much time I could spend with my family, what time I had to get up in the morning, and basically how to live my life.

I soon realized that corporate America would pay workers just enough so they wouldn't quit, and that workers in turn would work just hard enough not to get fired. If you can't say Amen, just say Ouch!

I prayed about my situation long and hard and asked God to put me in a financial position to be able to run my business full time, if that was His will. I consider it no coincidence that only a few weeks later, my corporate job hired a new vice president and he decided he wanted to run the company by himself rather than empowering the help of others. Long story short, I was either going to resign or get fired, because the tension in our relationship was so strong that one of us had to go. Well, I took that as my sign from God to make a choice, so I resigned from the company and punched my time clock for what I promised myself would be the last time.

I took a much-needed vacation with some friends and did a lot of soul-searching. I knew when the party was over I had no nice comfortable job to come back to, and I had some choices to make. I knew I wanted to run my own business and expand my current clientele, but the services I was offering did not generate enough income to support myself.

I asked myself what services I could offer that would coincide with the services I already offered, and in the process make me more money. The answer was clear—mortgage and real estate. There was just one small problem; I knew nothing about mortgage or real estate.

Instead of doing what most people do, which is go find another job, I chose not to give up on my dream.

Some people say it is not *what* you know, but *who* you know. Well, I disagree. I know the president of the United States, but he does not know me. I believe it is 10 percent what you know, 30 percent who you know, and 60 percent who knows you and is willing to help you.

With that in mind, I went to a friend who was a mortgage broker and asked him to teach me the mortgage business. He talked to me for half a day. He gave me enough information to hold a conversation with someone about mortgages, and he told me to go find someone looking for a house. I had no idea what I was doing, but I did what he told me to do for the next thirty days, and in the process earned approximately $5,000.

I was amazed at the good money, but I made perhaps the most common mistake in the mortgage business. I busted my pipeline. I got so focused on the one client I had, that I forgot to look for more clients. Long story short, I had no more clients and to survive I had to go find some more and start all over. During that time, I almost lost everything I owned. I had to move in with my girlfriend because I could not afford rent. My truck and my motorcycles almost got repossessed because I could not afford them. Everyone I knew, especially friends and family, told me I would never make it. They told me to give up on my silly dreams and go get a real job. The chips were down like never before.

The one thing that kept me going was my desire to succeed, and the choice I made was to win at all costs. My mother always told me that God will never put more on you than you can bear, but it sure felt like He was coming close! My Bible tells me that delayed doesn't mean denied. I did not feel God had brought me this far to leave me, so I was ready for the fight. Three months later, I closed a few deals all at once and carned almost $30,000 in one month! From that moment on, I told myself failure was not an option.

Three years later, my successes continue because I choose not to give up. The company I started is currently on pace to open fifty branch offices in Texas in the next one to two years. My successes have also blessed me to build a custom, seven-bedroom home for my family and to purchase a Jaguar, a Mercedes-Benz, and a Corvette. Those have long been my dream cars, and I chose to make my dreams come true.

Don't get me wrong; life is not all about the money. I did not come from money, so I know how to live without it. My motivating factor has always been success. I have always reached for the stars, even when the odds were against me. I knew once I achieved that level of success, the money would come, the freedom would come, and I would have the things I wanted in life.

Even though I have achieved a very high level of success at a very young age, the game is not over yet; I am just getting started. One of my good friends and mentors always says, "Success isn't in the destination, it's in the journey." Well, I am here to tell you my journey has just begun. I have a passion for helping others see their dreams come true. I want to show and empower as many people as I can, and let them know that they can win if they choose to do so. I want to show people there is a better way. I believe that the equation for success is: Preparation + Opportunity = Success. Are you prepared? Only you will know the answer to that question.

Life is all about choices. You are where you are today because of the choices you made in the last twelve months. By the same token, the choices you make today will determine where you will be in the next twelve months. In life, if you want something different, you have to do something different. It has been said, "If you always do what you have always done, you will always get what you always got". It's hard to lose when you have already made up your mind that you have won. In life, anything is possible, everything will get in your way, but nothing can hold you back.

Life is all about choices. Some are good, some are bad. Some are made for you, but most of them you make for yourself. When it comes down to it, you really only have two choices: You can make an excuse or you can make a change. I chose to make a change. How about you?

See you at the top!

About the Author

From growing up rummaging through slop barrels on the backs of farm trucks just to find his next meal; to now being included in the list of top 2 percent money earners in the country, it's no secret that Paul J. Brown, Jr. has came a long way. His life displays the image and gives a true testimony that success is possible if only you believe. Paul's biggest accomplishment, some would say, is that fact that he has never forgotten where he came from and what it took to make it. Paul is involved in numerous ministries helping young adults start off their personal and professional lives in a positive direction and also helping and families individuals twice his age restructure their game plan of life to achieve success. Paul has recently accepted his calling to the ministry to preach the word of God to those who believe and teach the word of God to those who don't have Christ in their lives. Paul is a true living example that anything is possible for those who believe.

For more information on Paul, please visit www.paulbrownjr.com, or contact him at 866.684.9946 or via e-mail at paul@paulbrownjr.com.

Chapter 12

Rising to the Challenge

EMMA PETERS

Ever since I answered life's most fundamental question—What is the purpose of my life?—I knew I would become very successful and have abundance in my life.

What came to me was the vision to build orphanages all over the world.

Rather than put this insight on the shelf for another day, I quit my job and launched an all-out, massive-action blitz to reach my company's Presidential level. Without looking back, I achieved that goal in just nine months.

Early on in my professional life, I had already committed to the welfare of children by choosing a career as a primary school teacher.

Indeed, well before starting my networking business, I had taken that commitment further by spending six months in Brazil working in a children's orphanage, and short periods of time on similar humanitarian projects in India and Mozambique.

I was drawn to teaching because I felt I could mold children's lives and change generations through them. Teaching is such an important job, and I loved it, but I also knew I could make an even bigger impact on the world if I utilized my talents in other ways. When I looked at my life's possibilities without the shackles of self-imposed limitations, I realized that, with financial freedom, I could make a large difference in the world.

The suffering of the third-world orphans I worked with made a lasting impression on me, inspiring me with their incredible courage, and delighting me with their endearing characters. I tapped a wellspring of motivation when I saw that my success offered a way to serve these children, even when I couldn't be present with them directly.

When you spend time with these children and see how they live on the streets, desperate for the next truck-load of rubbish and scraps full of flies, sniffing paint thinner to take the hunger away, smoking crack, stealing, prostituting themselves, sleeping huddled together underneath old blankets or cardboard, you can't help but ache for humanity. Such visions have never left me. The heartbreak of their plight made me realize that creating funds, building orphanages, and showering children in need with lots of love is my mission in life.

This realization came to me when I was living in London and earning roughly $1000 per month from my networking business. I flew to the States for my company's annual conference, and the words of one of the company's top leaders resonated in me.

He talked about the importance of believing in ourselves in order to be successful. He also said that, for things to change, we must change.

Rising to the Challenge

I decided to be one of those who takes the products and opportunity and make big things happen. I went home and took a financial risk by quitting my teaching position. Armed with a new level of belief, I drew energy for action from the act of burning my bridges.

I had a "big dream" board; I knew my goals (which were written down), and visualized them happening. By that point, I firmly believed I would succeed. Writing my goals and purposes clarified everything, the detail fueling my imagination. I quite literally saw and spoke myself to success!

I increased my belief by speaking out more than fifty affirmations every day in every aspect of my life, and putting my emotions into it. I even stated the date when I would receive a certain amount of money. I also verbalized the position I wanted to be in, my fitness goals, and my goals for relationships. I believe in the power of our words. As the scriptures say, there is life and death in the power of words, meaning our words have creative and destructive power. Each morning, I would get excited as I literally felt the emotion of being where I wanted to be and I stepped into my future!

The self-empowering affirmations propelled me to action. I utilized as wide a variety of outreach methods as I could, from basic person-to-person prospecting, to radio advertising, to a television interview with a doctor discussing my product line. Opportunities just kept coming my way. I believe these were in response to my strengthened faith. I was thrilled to accept an invitation from the same company leader who had so inspired me at the conference, to spend ten days of my blitz at his estate in Hawaii.

I utilized the time to the fullest, soaking up whatever I could in the form of mentoring and coaching, while also taking advantage of the chance to have such a successful and willing company leader talk to my prospects and conduct conference calls to aid the growth of my network.

It was incredibly powerful to be around him, and other extremely successful people. That trip proved very important for me personally as well as for my business.

Indeed, in the course of the nine months, I found myself evolving from a naturally shy person into a different person—more confident, more driven, more outgoing, more persuasive. As a consequence, I began attracting different types of people than I had as a part-time networker.

The result? Nine months after quitting my job, I had quadrupled my income. My organization grew not only in England, but also extended into the United States, Canada, and Australia as well. When I attended the annual company event the following year as a Presidential, I spoke in front of six-thousand fellow representatives—something I never could have imagined doing a short time before, because it would have been totally out of my comfort zone. One of my affirmations was seeing myself in front of thousands of people. Now it's millions. My next step is more radio and TV.

Expanding My Vision

When I outlined the vision that propelled me to Presidential, I set a goal of building five orphanages, beginning in India. Based on my prior work in orphanages, two strong convictions guided my thought process. First, I believe that children's greatest needs are for love, knowing God, a home, a sense of family, and improved nutrition. Second, I believe that a small home for orphans, where a group of twelve or fewer children live with a few adults caring for them, is a better setting for serving those needs than the larger institutions.

I decided the most effective role for me was to fund the construction of such homes where there were people in place who shared this vision, were willing and able to run them, and had the ability to fund ongoing operations. In addition, I would provide my company's nutritional products for children to each of the homes I built.

This approach allows me to leverage my funds and my efforts. Since I cannot be on-site in every location where I plan to build homes, finding local, like-minded partners can maximize the impact of the income I devote to the projects.

Fortunately, from my prior travels and church connections, I have enough contacts in and around the child welfare community, that finding trustworthy partners is the least of my concerns. Take, for example, the process through which I funded construction of my first orphan home last year in India, south of Bangalore. I started there because I have a close friend in the area who was an orphan himself, and had articulated a similar vision to me in the past.

My friend was brought up in a big institution, so he knows what it feels like not to have a family. I knew he had a goal of seeing small orphanages established all over India, so it was natural for us to join our visions together and support each other's goals.

There was already a building in place for girls at this site, and with my friend's organizational help, I funded construction of a companion building for boys, ages six to fourteen. I sent nutritional products, and have seen pictures of the completed structure and the boys who have moved in. Now, I have to plan a trip to see it up close.

Meanwhile, I am already in the planning phase of building a second home, also in India. In order to combine my vision with that of my contacts there, this project will be on a larger scale, aimed at housing fifty children, while still providing a home-style environment. In fact, I have no shortage of contacts in India, and could easily complete all the homes I envision in cooperation with them. Still, I have a strong desire to go into other countries as well, particularly Africa.

In the course of seeing the first home become reality, and laying groundwork for the second, two important things have occurred. I have expanded my initial goal of building five orphanages into a vision of building a hundred.

At first, five seemed like a huge goal, but my whole vision has progressed. I couldn't think on this scale before.

Perhaps even more importantly, I have inspired many others to share the vision and contribute their own efforts to it.

When people hear me talk about what we're doing, it causes them to realize they can do big things too. I urge them to identify and work toward realizing their visions, whether sharing in mine, or making their own a reality. I am working on a CD aimed at helping networkers do just that—live their dreams.

Setting a goal for beautiful properties, a new car, fit body, or luxury vacation is fine, but I encourage people to focus on their higher purpose.

I am particularly happy that my father, mother, and sister are actively involved in my business and my vision. Together, we set up a family charity called Acts One Eight (www.acts-one-eight.org) for collecting and distributing the funds with which the orphanages will be built. My sister recently reached the Presidential level herself, and my parents (who work in one distributorship as a team) are well on their way, too.

And now, others within my company have started coming forward to help fund the next home and the ongoing supply of nutritional supplements it will need.

I realize, of course, that to support this expanded vision, I have to generate substantially more income from my business and other supporters. Much like that initial nine-month action blitz that quadrupled my income, I am spending 2006 in the same mode, this time aiming for Platinum to match my business with the demands of my new goal.

Now that I've built one home, I know it can work. However, to reach my new goal, I'll have to build five or more per year. To do that, I need a business that can support multiple projects at once.

For me, this year is about balance; meeting my income goals has to be my focus. Then, the picture will change again and I'll spend more time traveling and making the necessary connections for setting up the orphanages.

I hope to inspire others to see that the real potential in leverage is not just the income it can help them produce in the business, but what they can *do* with that income. I'm capitalizing on that potential by leveraging my time, my income, and my network to make my vision reality.

In the end, success is about opening your eyes to what's possible and realizing you can actually achieve it, with God's help!

About the Author

Emma became a Christian while studying and working in Paris. She has a History of Art degree and a PGCE (Postgraduate Certificate in Education). She loves helping children —particularly orphans. Her Christian walk has taken her to Bible school, YWAM, and outreach in India, using puppets as a means of communicating the Gospel. Her travels have taken her to Argentina, where she visited Olmos maximum security prison, which was transformed into a model prison by a jailed Christian pastor. She has worked with Happy Child Mission in Bela Horizonte, Brazil, among some of the most deprived children in the world. She has witnessed firsthand the revival in Toronto, London, and Pensacola.

Two years ago, Emma decided to give up her job as a primary school teacher to work full-time as an independent associate of Mannatech Inc, a leading research and development company in the wellness industry specializing in glyconutrients. She is now a Presidential Director, and earns in two months what she previously earned in a year! This has changed her lifestyle dramatically, and given her the ability to travel extensively, help set up an orphanage, and provide nutritional products to medically fragile children around the world. Three Christmases ago, she traveled to an orphanage in Mozambique with life-giving glyconutrients for the children, some of whom were suffering with AIDS. Her travels have taken her all around the world, and she has recently returned from Hawaii following the Mannatech Presidential Summit. Her goal remains to help children regain good health, especially in the underprivileged parts of the world. Acts One Eight benefits enormously from her giving, and enables us to pioneer projects which normally would be left to others to do. For more information on Emma, please visit www.emmapeters.com or www.acts-one-eight.org, or e-mail her at emma@emmapeters.com.

Chapter 13

P.O.W.—The Power of Why!
Reasons Come First,
Answers Come Second!

DUG MCGUIRK

I have had the tremendous good fortune of being witness to some amazing success stories. In some respects, that's hardly unique; I assert that we all have been witness to success.

Even if we haven't witnessed the success firsthand, there is so much access to information these days that it's hard to miss a great story—especially when you are looking for it.

One of the most important things I have noticed is that the most successful people share a common trait: they have a compelling reason to do what they do or to be who they are.

Let's start with an example of the power of this phenomenon. Imagine you are climbing a mountain with a friend. You get to a steep ledge and need to get up and over it. The ledge you need to traverse is above your head, and you do not have much ground on which to stand. What will be the easiest way to get your friend over that ledge? Would it be easier for you to try to push and lift him over your head? What if your friend is bigger and heavier than you? Or would it be easier to grab him from above and pull him towards you? Well, I imagine is that pulling him up is going to be more effortless and effective. To stand on a precipice without good footing and try to lift or push a larger person over your head sounds like a losing proposition to me. I see that approach as being much like taking on a project or shooting for an outcome and not having a compelling "why" or reason to do it.

As it happens, one of my skill sets is that I can show you how to "WhyR" (wire) yourself such that you are excited to wake up each day and go for your outcome. Having a why for what you do will take you far. Sure, some people seem to be born with dumb luck, a horseshoe in one hand and a silver spoon in another. But in order to achieve continued success, you have to have a "why."

Following is an exercise demonstrating the pure power of having a "why." You will have an amazing experience if you really play with this. The gifts you will receive and the lessons you will learn from this exercise alone are more than worth giving it a shot!

1. Stand with your feet together, and take your right hand and point it forward. Next, keeping your feet flat and your arm straight, twist to your left as far as you comfortably can go, and see where you are pointing. Mark that spot in your mind. Twist back to where you started and drop your arm.

2. Now, close your eyes and visualize yourself twisting as you did before, only farther. In your mind's eye, twist completely in half. See that image of yourself clearly. Then see yourself twisting back to where you started, dropping your arm back to your side.

3. Once again, visualize yourself twisting with your arm. Clearly envision your arm pointing and your body twisting so far that your right arm is pointing more forward than if you would have just raised your right arm and pointed to the side. See, feel, and even hear yourself twisted that far—almost 360 degrees. Again, see, feel, and hear yourself twisting back to where you started from.

4. Try the visualization thing one last time, and make it crazy. See yourself, feel yourself, hear the sounds of your shirt and as you twist like a cartoon character all the way till you lap yourself and keep spinning like a corkscrew. Now see, hear, and feel yourself coming back in your mind's eye to your starting point, your arm back at your side.

5. Now it's time to actually raise your right arm and twist to your left as far as you comfortably can go, and notice how far you went.

When you do this, I am going to guess you are able to go a good 20–30 percent farther than you did the first time. Some will have gone even farther, depending on how vivid the visualization.

There are many lessons in that exercise, and in my book *Under Construction: Navigating the Detours on the Roads of Life*, I share a good deal of them. For now, let's say that how far you twisted in your mind is your reason, your why. The more compelling your why is, the more you can continue to focus on it and be motivated by it. That reason, or why, is going to keep you excited and inspired. And an added benefit is that it will motivate and inspire other people around you to support your cause. Without that motivator, you are in a boat without paddles, or on a bike without a chain. The reason is your fuel to get you to your destination.

I would like to share how powerful a why is from my personal experiences, and how it has enabled me to set a course and shape my life and journey. I have spent about fifteen years in the music business working on some amazing records. In that time, I have been a musical artist, performing on stage and making music; a producer; and an engineer, to name a few of my occupations.

For a variety of reasons, the music industry has been going through a tremendous paradigm shift. During this shift, I have watched many people succeed and even more fail. I have always had deep compassion for people, and witnessing the pain in this environment, and in others, caused me to reevaluate my position in life. I was also dealing with the changes in the music industry, and I needed to address my place in it.

I have never really been a "complainer." I will do my best to find what's great about a situation, and work to make it ever better. So I began to ask myself fundamental questions as I examined my journey thus far. Why do I do what I do? What rewards do I get from music and when I am most fulfilled in it? For what purpose have I spent all these years in such a chaotic industry? What needs of mine am I meeting?

I then broke down my various roles and explored my reasons. In other words, I explored how was I "WhyR'ed." In case you haven't noticed, all we do as human beings is ask questions anyway. Here is another one: Why not ask better questions?

The quality of your life is determined by the quality of your questions. If you ask poor questions you shall get poor answers. As the computer programmers say, garbage in; garbage out.

Now, this does not suggest that just asking a quality question is going to create a quality life. However, asking quality questions provides us with a tool to access a quality life—provided you answer them honestly. It also doesn't hurt to ask proactive, positive questions. For example, what am I most grateful for? What about that makes me feel so grateful? What am I most excited about? What about that makes me feel so excited? Who do I love? Who loves me? What can I do today to share my gifts and love with everyone I meet and enjoy the process?

Another key is to see the benefits of adversity. When faced with an obstacle, it is helpful to see the potential good that can come of the situation. You might ask yourself questions such as, What's great about this? What can I learn from this? What's funny about this? When asking these questions, of course, it's important that you honestly and truly answer them, and make the answers part of your being. In other words, asking and answering such questions is more than an intellectual exercise. You should *feel* your answers.

I started out as an artist and performer. The reward I got from that experience, my "why," was this: I had the amazing opportunity to connect with people. Offering a distraction for people as they went through the "rat race," and providing a great time made me feel great. I got to see it in real time, as it was happening. I felt I was contributing, helping people live fuller lives. As a creator, I would hear from people that my music helped them get through challenging times. I felt so honored to know that my existence and music were beneficial to others, and all I had to do was just be me. I recognized that the "space" I could provide people, the distraction, was an important distinction for me. One of my reasons was to provide a distraction or space for people to step out of their daily grind. Frankly, I also enjoy connecting with new people. I am "WhyR'ed" for that purpose.

As a producer/engineer, I met the "distraction" purpose just by participating in making music. When I would see a record I worked on selling in the multiple millions, I knew that I had done my part for all those people to have a better day. I was connected in some small way to everyone who enjoyed the record. When I hear songs I have worked on, or see videos, I still get that sense.

As a producer/mixer/engineer in the studio, my role is to understand what the artist wants, and do my part to make it a reality. It is so gratifying to be a part of that process. An artist has a vision or desired outcome for a sound, an energy or emotion that they want from the music. What I do is create the environment for that to become clear. Sometimes it's as simple as getting the right sound. Other times, it's the right instrument or arrangement. Sometimes it can be as complex as coaching the musician or artist to achieve an outstanding performance. When the project is complete, and the artist or band listens to the recording and says the result is better than they imagined, I am thrilled. I am "WhyR'ed" to create a space for transformation and the manifestation of new energy.

What I came to understand about myself and the rewards I received was profound, and gave me access to more resources within. Change is automatic, progress is not. For example, let's say you are driving down the road of life. You are headed west, and a detour sign appears. You take the detour, and it sends you south. You have now changed your direction, but are you still headed closer to your destination? Are you progressing towards your desired outcome? What I mean by this is that all actions will lead to change, but not all change is progress. I needed to control my focus. I realized that my purpose in music was to:

A. Provide a distraction for people, give them a chance to get out of their own ways and enjoy life.

B. Provide and create a space for achieving a vision.

C. Connect with people in person.

D. Travel.

Now for me, those were some huge distinctions. I finally understood what needs and whys were being met and things started to get clear. My next question was, "Is there more to this experience, and what would make this even more exciting and compelling?" As I pondered this, I realized that creating a distraction wasn't good enough for me. I love entertaining and being part of that process. I was, however, more excited when I thought about what would happen if, while I created a distraction, I could provide some "learning" so that when someone goes back to their "rat race," they could enjoy it. Or better yet, discover that they didn't need to go back into that race.

These thoughts got me so excited that I started exploring other opportunities and energies. One thing that came crashing into my mind was the idea of motivational speaking. I could entertain, use music, and put on a show while at the same time offer tools that could be applied when participants went home. I could travel to different cities and places just like when I toured. I would meet, connect, and learn from new people around the world. Would I have to give up music? Not at all! I can, do, and will still use its power to create "distraction" and "learning" or "conditioning." I can still make, perform, and otherwise create experiences with music—all in alignment with my goals.

Another opportunity came to mind in the form of coaching. We all have desired outcomes, yet sometimes we don't know how to achieve them. If you think of life as a game and you are willing to get on the field to play, not just be a spectator, you will notice that a coach is necessary. Examine, for a moment, professional sports. Every sport has a coach. From golf and tennis, to team sports, inevitably there are coaches offering objective guidance and expertise. In music production, my style has been that of a coach. Most of my experience in production has been with bands. As a producer, my role was to understand the "goal" and help the artists achieve it. I assisted in both the big picture and minor details, so they could concentrate on what steps needed to take place and be the best they could be. I worked to create a space so that the music could flow the most creatively, leading to the ultimate vision. Now, I do that not just for bands, but for regular people as well.

I also have created some methods to positively bring about paradigm shifts in human consciousness through other forms of media. Using the skill sets I have learned, and continue to learn, I have created a multimedia experience to provide the opportunity for people to discover what they want in life. This was another benefit arising from my ability to understand why I do anything. Knowing what my needs were was paramount to discovering what other opportunities were present. I believe that success in anything comes in direct proportion to the clarity of your why, which in turn will give you access to clarity of your vision. Or, said another way, we all do things for a purpose and when we clearly know what that purpose is, we can then figure out the how. The how will show itself soon after we discover the compelling why. The universe is funny that way. It only knows how to fulfill clear requests.

Affecting people on a mass scale was always important to me. I realized that when I asked myself why I enjoyed working on such big records. Knowing that I worked on a record that sold tens of millions of copies made me happy. I realized that the more records were sold, the more people I touched in my own little way. I recognized that I wanted to affect the masses. I already knew that I love performing in front of large crowds—the bigger the better.

I share these personal experiences to show just some examples of how you can examine your surroundings and choices in an effort to create the life you desire. I believe that it is absolutely possible to live a joyful and fulfilled life doing whatever you want. From my humble perspective, I found that knowing how I am "WhyR'ed" offered tremendous power to uncovering opportunity. I have found it to be a consistent thread of energy among successful people. Success, to me, is living a life that is joyful and fulfilled. A life of action full of mistakes is far better than a life of inaction full of regrets.

As I conclude, I would like to offer two wise statements. My intention in sharing these sayings is to offer some strength and things to think about. They have been very powerful for me.

The first is, "If you are willing to do only what's easy, life will be hard. But if you are willing to do what's hard, life will be easy." I noticed that when I broke through some of my fears regarding networking and meeting people, a whole new world opened up for me. I used to find it very difficult to meet new people and connect with them. Now, connection is one of my greatest joys. I have made some of my most powerful connections from being willing to stretch myself and do something I thought was very hard. Another perspective is this: People can choose to take an easy path of just living day-by-day, not growing or challenging themselves or contributing in any meaningful way to society. If one spends his life doing what's convenient and comfortable he will be doing so for his entire life and wind up dead, or dead broke. Conversely, if one works really hard at developing himself or a business, he can create an extraordinary life that comes naturally. The chains of habit are too light to be felt until they are too heavy to be broken. I suggest you look closely at your life and ask yourself where you are taking the easy path, why, and where that path is leading you.

The second quote is this: "You don't have to get it right, you just need get it goin'!" That, to me, has many meanings. One is that action is better than no action. It's a quick way to move away from the paralysis of analysis. Also, we know from physics that things in motion stay in motion, while things at rest stay at rest. Now, I am not suggesting we all take action without thought. It is so important to use your sensory acuity. That is to say, it is important to take notice of what is working and what is not, and to adjust accordingly. Again, like a detour on your road, notice if your actions are taking you to your desired outcome. This is a paramount point in regard to strategy. It's a lot easier to adjust to a situation if you are dealing with it, as opposed to being blindsided or kicked by it. In my book, *Under Construction: Navigating the Detours on the Roads of Life*, I use the analogy of the road being our path. If you are in a moving car, it's easier to turn the wheel and navigate around something than if the car is stationary.

Simply by purchasing and reading this book, you are farther along your path to success than you can imagine. Studies have shown that just 80 percent of books that are purchased are ever read completely. So many people don't finish what they start, failing to recognize that the success they seek is tantalizingly close. At least 80 percent of success is just showing up. The remainder comes from sticking with it. By reading this book, you have demonstrated that you are playing the game on the field. I am confident you will succeed—provided you stay the course.

About the Author

Dug is a seasoned insider working in the music industry for more than fifteen years. He has real experience on both sides of the studio glass. Starting out as an intern, he immersed himself in a company that was functioning as a production company, record label, publishing company, and a commercial recording studio. During his tenure, Dug has worked on some of the biggest albums of the '90s. Dug has coproduced and imaged radio programs for ABC radio, as well as voiced commercials. He has performed as a solo artist and in several bands at many levels from touring to recording. At the same time, Dug has established himself as an engineer/producer with an impressive and extensive discography under his own company, Thru the Din Productions. His full and rich experiences in such a wide range in the industry give him unique insights to support artists. Wearing his acting hat, Dug has appeared in a few movies, commercials, and music videos.

Dug is also a certified Master Practitioner of Neuro Linguistic Programming (NLP) and a doctoral candidate in psycho neurology and alterative medicine. He is a speaker reaching and touching many with the message of The Power of Words and The Power of Why. Having succeeded in achieving so much in the music industry, Dug has had the opportunity to befriend other very successful people, and learn what makes them tick. Through the various NLP technologies, Neuro Stratology, and new Psycho Neurological technologies, Dug has been able to uncover models of success and master the art of sharing this information through various methods, such as speaking, writing, and the media.

As a Life Coach Dug, has engaging conversations leading to massive action, generating powerful momentum, achieving incredible results. Dug will show you all you need is within you now and you do indeed have access to it all!

For more information, visit www.thruthedin.com or e-mail dug@thruthedin.com.

Chapter 14

Winning Is a Habit, and so Is Losing

ANTONIO ADAIR

Have you ever wondered why some people just always seem to win? It's as if everything they touch seems to turn to gold and they have what we call the Midas touch. While on the other hand, others can never seem to get it right. They couldn't get a weed to grow. They would actually kill it while trying to get it to grow. What is the difference between these two types of people? They have both formed habits. One has formed good habits, and the other bad habits. Sounds very minute, but over a period of time, the habits we form will make a **huge** difference in our lives.

Some of us are in the habit of making excuses and others are in the habit of getting results. One bad habit that some people have is watching twenty-seven hours of television per week. Why not pick up a book and read? We could consider that a good habit, could we not? But we would all rather go to the movies than to the library, because it is easier to **entertain** ourselves than it is to **educate** ourselves. If we could take half of those hours that we are watching television, and instead educate ourselves with something that we want to be better in or need to be better in, just imagine how much we could improve in one year. Another bad habit is having the wrong conversations with ourselves. I once read that there's a part of our mind that does not like us, *The Emotional Prisoner by Jose Villegass III*. Sounds strange, but it is the truth. Think about that for a moment. Are you in the habit of letting the part of your mind that does not like you talk you out of things that you should be talking yourself into? If we don't take control of that part of our mind, it will always control us.

Are you in the habit of executing or procrastinating? When you have a deadline, or something you need to complete, do you put it off until the last minute, or do you jump all over it? Brian Tracy has a great book on procrastination, titled *Eat That Frog*, which is a great read in the process of educating ourselves. That makes the difference between winning and losing.

Other bad habits that we have are getting advice from the worst sources possible. Why is it that we take advice from people who are in worse situations than we are. Sometimes we are willing to take business advice from those who have never run a business (or a successful business). What a bad habit that is. We are also willing to take financial advice from people who are, by no stretch of the imagination, anywhere near being financially fit or free. Why does the opinion of those who are in no position to give any advice matter to us? I learned years ago to never ask anyone their opinion if they did not have anything that I wanted. Doesn't it make more sense to ask a successful business person for their opinion about a business investment. The same would apply to our finances.

Another bad habit that we have—and we may not even consider this a bad habit—the company we keep. You can learn a lot about a person from the type of people they allow to be in their company. Our friends are like buttons on elevators, some of them will take us UP, and some of them will take us DOWN. What most people do not realize is that to have a lifestyle improvement, they have to get the Wrong people out of their lives in order for the Right things to happen. But we sometimes make the mistake of hanging out with people we are bigger than. It makes us feel good to have others look up to us in the circle that we run in. Instead of us keeping people around us who can stretch us and make us grow, we have the bad habit of keeping people around us who prevent our growth.

A winning habit would be keeping people around us who are doing a lot better than we are, so we are always being stretched. Be the weakest link, not the strongest. For example, if we are blessed to where we are earning a six-figure yearly income, a goal of ours should be to seek the company of people who are making six-figures a month. Imagine all the stretching we'd go through if we were in that type of company. Who would not want to be in that company, if they were truly trying to grow and become better? Once again, this would be the mindset of someone who is in the habit of winning. Show me your *friends* and I will show you your *future*. They say that we are the average of our five closest friends. Think about your five closest friends—are they in the habit of winning or losing? Whoever they are, that's who you are.

The difference between winning and losing is overcoming the temptation of quitting. Most people are *professionals* when it comes to starting things, but *amateurs* when it comes to finishing them. Sometimes, we as people tend to give up on things too easily. To be a winner is to be a finisher. Dewayne Wade and Lebron James are spectacular with their moves on the basketball court and we can say they are both in the habit of winning as well. In addition to being winners, they are also great finishers. Think about it this way, both these NBA superstars can do unbelievable things to get to the basket and score. We have seen basketball players make a great move toward the basket and we oo and ah about that move, but then they miss the shot. The move was so good they should have received two points for the move itself. But they were unable to finish and no points were scored because it does not matter how great the move was: all that matters is that they were able to finish.

As adults, we sometimes contradict ourselves when it comes to quitting or giving up. We push our kids and encourage them to always complete whatever they start. "Never give up" is what we say to them. We've said things like "If you quit now, you will be quitting things for the rest of your life." Some of us as parents have even gone as far as telling our children they don't have a choice in the matter, they will finish or else. Sound familiar? Now, it's funny how we'll push our kids to finish, but we are quick to walk away from things ourselves. We need to take heed of our own advice. Why do we say these things to our children? Because we do not want them forming bad habits and getting into the habit of losing. We want them to be winners. So, before we walk away from our next incomplete assignment, let's think about what we expect from our children. And always remember this: winners do what they have to do and losers do what they want to do.

For some, unfortunately, life will be about inconvenience, not convenience. Sometimes we are forced to grow because of our circumstances and most of us were not born with silver spoons in our mouths. They say pain is a gift that nobody wants. Who really sees pain as a gift? Yet without pain, we would not know what adjustments or changes to make. We would continue to do the same things over and over. We would never learn from our mistakes.

Jose Villegas would say that pain is necessary, but suffering is optional. One bad habit we have is suffering more than we have to. In business, or in our personal lives, we tend to do just that, we suffer more than we have to. A lot of times we know when things are not good for us, but we just opt to suffer and endure the pain that we are going through, and it turns into suffering—definitely a bad habit. Ask yourself, what are you enduring at this time in your life that you know is not good for you or anyone else, but you have elected to suffer because you fear the unknown. In life, there is no growth without pain! Just remember that the suffering is optional. So, in other words stop suffering and move on!

Having a plan or goal is a good habit. We've all heard the saying that goes if you don't have a plan, then you plan to fail. Why is it that when people want something, or want to accomplish something, they do not put a plan in place? Having a plan or putting goals in place is basically preparing for the future. Most people don't look at things this way. When we have those plans and goals, and we are working towards them, it allows us to pull our future into the present. That's a good habit to have, wouldn't you agree?

I was in the Midwest a few years ago, when I wandered into a Wal-Mart. I can spend hours in Wal-Mart just, walking around and buying things. Remember this while you are on your way to millions, that it's not about how much you make, it's about how much you keep—a good habit to have. I had gone into Wal-Mart somewhere around 2:00 a.m. and there was an older woman there who was greeting customers. She had to be in her late seventies to early eighties and I asked myself, was she there because she wanted to be, or was it because she had to be? If she was there because she had to be, I said to myself, there is a person who did not plan or have goals (or the wrong goals). Now don't get me wrong, I know some people love what they do, but to do it at 2:00 a.m. at her age? I know there are a lot of other things she could be doing at that hour, like sleeping for instance!

Just think about all the people across the world who have no plans or goals, and end up that same way. Or think about it this way, when was the last time you walked into Wal-Mart and had a teenager say to you "Welcome to Wal-Mart?" Normally it's someone who is in their golden years in those types of positions. Poor planning or lack of planning will always be disastrous—a bad habit. What is so unfortunate is that people will read this book and do nothing about changing their habits.

In life the only that is consistent is change. In a few years, we'll all be saying "Do you remember when gas was $3.00 per gallon in 2006." I remember in 1991 when I was getting out of the Navy and SUPER was only $1.20 per gallon. So, knowing that change is the only thing that is consistent years from now, will you be in a better place because you started to form good winning habits or will you be in the same place you are now because you could not change your bad habits?

In life, the decisions we make are critical to our progression or digression. So, from this point on in our lives let's try to form better habits and do more winning. Lets continue to press on with whatever we are going through. Some of these things will be painful, but our goal or plan is to get better and stronger in this process, and to form better habits. Let's not quit when the going gets tough, because though **it will not be easy** as we move forward, **it will be worth it**. Make a decision that you will not throw the towel in from the experiences that we have just grown from. That's a bad habit and that's exactly what we are trying to change and improve about ourselves. As we go through life, we will continue to win or lose, and the thing that will determine the difference will be the habits we create and break along the way. It is that simple, so remember that, and keep it that simple. Winners do what they have to do and losers do what they want to do! So as winners let's not just take care let's go and take charge!

1. Read.

2. Control the part of your mind that does not like you.

3. Eat that frog (stop procrastinating and execute).

About the Author

Antonio Adair has changed his life and the lives of many others through the Network Marketing industry. A few years ago, he decided to join the Network Marketing industry and his life changed overnight. Although he was a small business owner and a supervisor for the US Postal Service, he still found himself financially challenged and overwhelmed. Twenty-five thousand dollars in credit card debt, chased by the student loan mafia, and driving a nice, shiny Lexus, but unable to afford automobile insurance was an indication that something had to change.

Financial problems are now in the distant past. Antonio has built teams numbering in the tens of thousands, and his organization now spans the entire globe. As a highly sought-after success coach and motivational speaker, Antonio has quickly become a leader in the industry. One of his proudest achievements in life is being able to retire his mother—a dream that he only thought possible by becoming either a professional athlete or an entertainer. Because of the Network Marketing industry, Antonio's mother has not worked a job in seven years!

Although naturally shy and introverted, Antonio has learned how to become a "situational extrovert." Operating outside of his comfort zone has truly paid off for Antonio. It is this unique ability to truly empathize with those who do not possess an outgoing personality that allows Antonio to connect in a special way with others.

Multiple Streams of Inspiration

Having achieved the pinnacle of success, Antonio wants to share this gift with as many others as possible. Antonio's dynamic training sessions, passionate coaching, and master strategies are a true indicator of the many individuals whom he has assisted in living their dreams.

For more information, please e-mail Antonio at: aadair@antoniosadair.com.

Chapter 15

Do You Have the Will to Live?

Chad & Tracie Czerneski

"Loss or Gain, Joy or Pain, Success or Defeat, Life or Death, The choice is yours!" —*Chad Czerneski*

Chad: While working hard to ensure the mail would get out in time, I caught a glimpse of an angel out of the corner of my eye. I proclaimed aloud at that instant "Now that is the woman I have been searching for all my life, and she will become my wife." A few looked at me like I was crazy, but those who really knew me knew that there was truth in what I had just said. I quickly introduced myself as "the man you will marry and fall in love with, you just don't know it yet." We met in October, and by the following June we were married. Everything since the day we met was like a real-life fairy tale that ended happily ever after. Then, we hit a major road bump. Have you ever had just one those days, weeks, or years? Have you heard the expression when it rains it pours?

Well, just two weeks after our wedding, the "I do" became a quick "Death do us part!" Tracie was told, "I am sorry, but your husband has stage 4 bone cancer and is going to die! He has six weeks to six months, if he is lucky!" We were also told I was 100 percent incapable of ever being able to have future children. School has been easy for both of us, so no test had ever been this difficult. We first thought, *There is no way this is really happening to us; quick, pinch me—are we dreaming? Ouch. I felt that and it's defiantly not a dream.* The news grew worse and worse with each passing day. The doctors determined the cancer had been there for at least seven to ten years. Chemotherapy would have to be started immediately and since we both had full-time jobs at the time, we both took a leave of absence to make the long five-hour drive to the Cleveland Clinic from Michigan to begin the treatment. When we arrived, we were told that if I survived and if we ever wanted to have children, we would need to visit the sperm bank and freeze some samples because the cancer and the treatment would definitely make me 100 percent sterile. We ended several months of chemotherapy, often with my throwing up the entire way home to Michigan, only to be admitted to the emergency room for dehydration. Then it was time to turn around and come back for more chemo.

Tracie: After three months, the treatment was deemed ineffective, and it was determined it would be necessary to remove Chad's leg. Being a nationally ranked boxer and a very competitive athlete, this news almost destroyed his spirit. But his sheer will and determination to keep his leg convinced the doctors to save the it. The surgery would be in one week, and we now had to arrange for more time off work and try to figure out some way to pay our bills. It was at this point that the credit card debt started to rack up. Missing so much work, we had already gone through all our savings and cashed in all of our CDs and savings bonds. At such a young age we never planned for this sort of thing to happen. *Hint: plan for emergencies, by creating an emergency fund.*

Chad had some leave time left, but ultimately I had no choice but to quit my job. Chad felt terrible, but I joked with him that I never really like the job in the first place.

We were both single parents when we met, with neither of the other biological parents in either child's life, and our children were both entering kindergarten in less than one week. Thankfully, our parents were willing to make the necessary arrangements to make themselves readily available to help with the children, to whom we are ever grateful. The hotel, food, and gas bills were adding up fast. I began living on Visa today, MasterCard tomorrow, using the Discover to pay the bills at home and saved the American Express for emergencies. After several months of commuting from state to state and hospital to hospital the credit cards had all reached their limit and my body had reached its limit as well. I was lacking sleep and my stomach thought it was in the Twilight Zone from all the hospital and fast food. I went to the hospital chapel and prayed for a miracle every night, and we got some assistance from friends and family, for which we were very grateful. One night, the boys were crying of hunger pangs, and as I went to the refrigerator, I saw there was nothing to feed them that morning. I then swallowed my pride and did what was necessary to feed my children. I was forced to do the unthinkable—apply for welfare and food stamps. I remember Chad telling me that we needed to do whatever it took to get through this, because he would conquer this cancer and we would once again have our fairy tale.

So, as Chad had done so many times before, I proclaimed aloud that our being broke was just a temporary situation and that we would pull through.

Next came the operation. After eight hours of surgery, the team of doctors came and told me that it was much worse than they had thought, and they had to remove two-thirds of the muscle from Chad's leg, bottom, and lower back, along with a major portion of the left side of his pelvic bone. The doctors then told me to go back to the hotel. When I arrived, there was a red flashing light on my phone and I thought, "Who has left me a message?" It was the hospital calling to say Chad had died, his heart stopped from an overdose of morphine after the surgery, but not to report to the hospital because Chad had been revived and he would be in ICU for close monitoring and everything was now all right.

The surgery was not a success. We were told after the report came back, the negative margins were not negative, and contained cancer as well. Chad now had an internal infection which required an additional two-week hospital stay. The next step was six weeks of radiation treatments, with little success. Chad was sent home with a morphine drip and an in-home nurse.

After months of struggling with illness, poverty, a new marriage, and our ready-made family, at times we all wondered where we were being led and why. What was to come and where did our future lie? Was it going to be "Loss or Gain, Joy or Pain, Success or Defeat, Life or Death?"

Chad: One day, while lying in bed, I realized this was a test and that my fight was not over yet. I prayed and thanked my Lord and Savior for the wonderful life He had given me; I asked for forgiveness for my past sins and for direction in creating a better life for my family, the world, and myself. At this point, an Anthony "Tony"

Robbins infomercial was on the television. Thinking, *Well I don't need any motivation to die*, I began to reach for the remote control, when the infomercial claimed that for an extra fee you could have lunch with boxer "Sugar" Ray Leonard. The light came on in my head, and I knew I needed to see him before I died. With that thought, I called to my wife "Honey, we're going to an Anthony Robbins event and I am going to meet "Sugar" Ray Leonard.

Tracie: At this point, I thought he had lost his mind and wondered how I was I going to get him into a wheelchair with his IV. We didn't have any money, but I knew if he said we were going, he meant it, and he would find a way. Remember that American Express card? I didn't, but Chad did, and we booked two tickets. The day of the event, Chad disconnected the IV and I put him in a wheelchair. When we got to the event we discovered there was no wheelchair access to the seats we had purchased. I felt awful, but I knew we had to leave. Chad said "no way" and demanded we buy a pair of crutches from the drugstore nearby. He forced himself onto the crutches with sincere determination—wobbling and sweating from pure pain—and we made our way into the Palace of Auburn Hills.

As always, Mr. Robbins outdid himself by over-delivering his message. The presentation was phenomenal and inspiring, but all Chad wanted to do was get to lunch with his inspiration and role model in the sport of boxing—"Sugar" Ray Leonard. When the time came, Chad worked his way up to the lunch area. By the time we arrived most of the seats were taken. Do you believe that everything in life happens for a reason? Well, quantum physics states . . . OK we won't go into that, but Chad sat next to a well-dressed man, and I sat in the last seat to the left of Chad. The gentleman was Roger Leonard, Sugar's brother, who had also boxed for the United States Air Force. Chad smiled for the first time in a long time. We took pictures with Roger and Ray, and Chad got his boxing gloves signed by Ray. This seemed to bring some color into Chad's face for the first time in months. He was so inspired by meeting and speaking to his role model that we went and finished listening to the remainder of the seminar.

When we got back from lunch, Anthony mentioned some health challenges of his that were reversed by alkalizing his blood and body by raising his pH. He went on to tell the story of a boy with "Glass Bone Disease," who had also reversed his health challenges by raising his body's pH. This immediately grabbed our attention. We thought bone—bone cancer? Maybe this is the real reason we are here. We rushed as fast as Chad could crutch along to the back of the room and tried to purchase the products to raise pH.

After trying several credit cards, we finally found one that was accepted. We went directly home and Chad began using the product.

Chad: Remarkably, in three days, the seven-year heartburn was gone and I started to feel much better. I had better clarity, was needing less sleep, and the pain was less severe. I knew there was something to this "raise the pH" product and lifestyle. I began to research via the phone and Internet everything I could find about pH. There wasn't a lot of information available, but I read it all. The product we had purchased was expensive, and I was running out fast. I was able to find the address and phone number of the company that made the product, and I gave them a call.

The company was a nonprofit organization based in Utah, and for a nominal fee, I could receive the product at a lower cost. It meant we could afford to buy more.

After a few short weeks, my health began to take a miraculous turn. I was feeling less fatigued each day, losing weight, and trying to walk with the assistance of a walker.

Tracie: I saw an incredible change in Chad's attitude toward life, and he proclaimed for all to hear "I am going to beat this cancer. I am going to live and I am going to walk again, you watch." I knew that somehow, everything would soon be OK, and I would have my husband back. More importantly, our children would have a father once again. Chad removed the IV of morphine, and quickly moved from a walker, to crutches, to a cane.

Not long after this, the phone rang. A man named Kevin (who has become a mentor and dear friend to both of us since) stated the company was no longer a nonprofit, and that a well-known, publicly traded company had purchased the marketing rights to it. He stated 'Tracie Czerneski' was in the system as a distributor, and we now had the opportunity to make money simply by sharing our story of how this product had helped Chad.

Have you ever heard something that sounded too good to be true?

Well we had too, but this seemed different, and almost overnight, people started asking us about the amazing transformation of Chad's health, and we started telling them all we knew. Chad told me he was familiar with this type of business opportunity and that it could get us out of debt, give us a chance to make a living from home, and stay at home with our children. I knew nothing of MLM (multi-level marketing) other than what I had witnessed with my own eyes of Chad making the impossible possible by beating this disease.

To date, the organization has taken on a life of its own, with distributors sharing the word of health and wealth by simple raising your pH. It has grown to 25,000 distributors worldwide, bringing in close to $100,000 in volume each week. At one point, our finances had gotten so bad, we had to file bankruptcy and apply for food stamps but now the household income has reached a serious six figures, and we have made over a million dollars since this life-changing, life-altering experience enhanced our lives. Like Chad says, it wasn't a disease it was an *opportunity* to change not only our health, but our wealth as well.

If you remember the beginning of this chapter, we were told by several different sources that Chad would be sterile and not able to have children, ever, 100 percent sterile. Well, if we were to allow other's perceptions to become our reality we would now still be happily married with our two children. But we create our own future because we know that ultimately we are the only ones who must make things happen, and this knowledge has allowed us to grow stronger each day. I can proudly say that Chad proclaimed aloud that he would give me the daughter I always wanted, and within months I conceived our son—well he was close. I went in for my six-week check-up after the baby came, and the doctor said, "The baby is very healthy, and you are very pregnant," and soon after I found out it was with our beautiful baby girl.

The man who was dealt the fate of death demanded a new life, which he now has. He has been able to not only watch but also participate in raising our children and passing on his life experiences in sports, education, and overcoming adversity of all types. Chad has successfully removed the word "quit" from the Czerneski dictionary, and this has allowed our children to excel in all they do. In fact, our four children are all national-level athletes. Chad and I speak to children and parents all over the world, teaching them that the key to overcoming any and all obstacles in life is simply a combination of continued education and taking control of your destiny.

Chad's health has returned, and he is a better man today than he ever was prior to this "near death experience." As Chad likes to say (he likes to say a lot!) winners never quit, winners never give up, and winners never die! Never lose the faith, Never lose hope.

Always look to better yourself from one day to the next, and you will continue to grow. No one else can do it for you. Only you can make it happen, you're the only one who can live your life and your life will be what you make of it. Nothing good ever happens by itself. If you want the right things to happen, you must, by way of your own actions, create them. Do right things, and make them always honorable, and the right things will happen in return. Success of any kind is a four-letter word, W-O-R-K. Anyone who is willing to do this will win the game of life.

Life is real, and the grave is not your goal so live, love, and allow yourself to be loved. Enjoy every aspect of your life, and most important, allow your children to be children and cherish every moment you breathe the same air they do.

Chad: If we had allowed others' perceptions to become our reality, I would not be here today. Tracie and I did not choose this option, instead we chose LIFE! Proclaiming your intention aloud is a key point to turning your thoughts into reality.

About the Authors

Chad and Tracie have been happily married for over seven years, and are the proud parents of four wonderful children—three boys and one girl. Their vast experience and education make them a truly unique couple. Chad's background has taken him all over the world, and he and Tracie have pulled from their experience in both corporate America and as entrepreneurs to become personal development and leadership coaches and motivational speakers. They would love to help men and women all over the world become stay-at-home moms and dads! For more information on Chad and Tracie, please visit www.RaiseYourPH.com or call 1-877-RaiseYourPH.

Chapter 16

Bringing Success Home
A Business Woman's Guide To Success

TUNITA BAILEY

What is true success?

For me, success was once defined as money, material possessions, and acquiring real estate. I worked long hours, and if I wasn't at the office, my mind was. Every evening, after picking up my kids Jasmine, four and Jade, three, we would stop by McDonald's or Wendy's and pick up dinner and go back to the office to work until 9:00 or 10:00 at night, or until the kids fell asleep. If my actions were questioned, I quickly responded that my kids and husband would enjoy the money, and I would feel the success from the fruits of my labor.

Today, I realize that success is what money cannot buy. It is the fruits of the spirit. It is your health, your strength, your joy, your peace within, and overall happiness in life. It is the smile on your child's face as you accompany her on a field trip for school, or the surprise in your husband's eyes when you show up at his job just to say hello. Is success preparing a favorite meal for your family to enjoy, or a vacation at Disney World? Could it be defined as simply a drive down to the resort in Florida for a weekend of fun and games?

Success Defined

Success is defined as the achievement of something desired, planned, or attempted.

Success can be things you desire, such as becoming a millionaire, or making just enough to pay your bills; it can be defined as living in a multimillion-dollar estate on a hill, or simply a comfortable and cozy home in the suburbs. It can also be described as owning a brand new Mercedes or simply an older Mustang that is paid for.

Success can be planned around things you want to happen at a later date. An example of planned success could be a child's graduation after twelve long years of school, planning a marriage to your significant other, or planning a vacation.

Success can be something you attempted to do but did not complete as you had planned, such as attempting to lose one hundred pounds and only losing ten.

Understanding true success means realizing what your definition is and focusing on fulfilling the passions of your life.

There was famous singer named Billie Holliday. Her life story was portrayed by Diana Ross in *Lady Sings the Blues* (1972). Billie Holliday pursued what she believed was success by trying to sing her way to the top. Without regard to whom she hurt or left behind, she was determined to make it to the top. Once she achieved her goal of becoming a success, she quickly realized that there was no one there to enjoy it with. And as Billy Dee Williams said, in *Mahogany* (1975), "Success is nothing without someone to share it with."

So many women strive to be successful in life by trying to achieve material things. We often don't realize that true success is shared with those you love.

I don't believe that anyone on their deathbed has ever said "I wish I had spent more time at the office." As a matter of fact, they would probably say "I wish I had spent more time at home. I should have spent more time with my family."

If you were at the end of your journey, and were able to look back at all you had accomplished in life up to this point, would you consider yourself a success, and would it feel like home.

S*U*C*C*E*S*S

S—Secretly understanding your passion in life

U—Using your knowledge and experience to direct your path

C—Continuing to seek wisdom

C—Counting your blessings

E—Enjoying life with those you love

S—Spending quality time with yourself

S—Saving money for your future

The Woman's Role in the Home

As a woman in business, my role at the office had an impact on my role as a wife and mother at home. The role of business owner required me to constantly think about how to increase production. My job description included recruiting, training, and managing employees. One of the most challenging aspects of ownership is recruiting and retaining good employees. It seemed as seen as a good employee was hired and trained, they would often leave the company for a better opportunity. This would often disturb the flow of production and affect the harmony of the office. As an effective owner and manager, my role was to keep the goals and objectives of the organization on track.

A woman's role in the home is just as demanding. As women, we are commanded to take care of ourselves, respect our husbands, nurture our children, and be great businesswomen. We must own and manage ourselves in order to assure the productivity of the family. Our spouse should be able to trust our decisions, and know that we are being loyal, dedicated, and committed to excellence. Our children should understand the importance of independence, responsibility, and contentment.

My favorite verse in the Bible is Proverbs 31, verses 10–31

> 10 A wife of noble character who can find? She is worth far more than rubies.

> 11 Her husband has full confidence in her and lacks nothing of value.

> 12 She brings him good, not harm, all the days of her life.

> 13 She selects wool and flax and works with eager hands.

14 She is like the merchant ships, bringing her food from afar.

15 She gets up while it is still dark; she provides food for her family and portions for her servant girls.

16 She considers a field and buys it; out of her earnings she plants a vineyard.

17 She sets about her work vigorously; her arms are strong for her tasks.

18 She sees that her trading is profitable, and her lamp does not go out at night.

19 In her hand she holds the distaff and grasps the spindle with her fingers.

20 She opens her arms to the poor and extends her hands to the needy.

21 When it snows, she has no fear for her household; for all of them are clothed in scarlet.

22 She makes coverings for her bed; she is clothed in fine linen and purple.

23 Her husband is respected at the city gate, where he takes his seat among the elders of the land.

24 She makes linen garments and sells them, and supplies the merchants with sashes.

25 She is clothed with strength and dignity; she can laugh at the days to come.

26 She speaks with wisdom, and faithful instruction is on her tongue.

27 She watches over the affairs of her household and does not eat the bread of idleness.

28 Her children arise and call her blessed; her husband also, and he praises her:

29 "Many women do noble things, but you surpass them all."

30 Charm is deceptive, and beauty is fleeting; but a woman who fears the lord is to be praised.

31 Give her the reward she has earned, and let her works bring her praise at the city gate.

As a Proverbs 31 woman, we must do the following:

Be of noble character and be worth more than rubies.

A woman's first responsibility is to have good character. Be a woman who is trustworthy, loyal, and committed to excellence. Your value should be worth more than rubies. Your husband should be able to completely trust your judgment in matters of the home. He should have the confidence in you that will allow him to be a great leader.

Make your selections carefully and prepare ahead of time.

When you are shopping, choose wisely the best food and clothing for the family. Your children will desire fast foods and want to eat out, however, you must have the better judgment and require them to eat at home as often as possible. It is perfectly acceptable in today's society to eat out once or twice a week. As women we have such busy schedules and often it saves us the time of cooking.

One technique for assuring the family eats at home is to prepare a weekly menu. In the morning, you can take out a chicken or roast, and slow cook it in your Crock-Pot. Voïlá! Dinner is ready when you get home. Eating out should be viewed as a treat and not as the norm for your family.

Your daughters will want to shop and spend money every weekend; you must teach them the value of taking care of what they have, and to be content. When they shop encourage them to buy quality, not quantity. Be diverse with the selection of clothing and shoes.

Be decisive, and a good manager of money.

If you see a great deal on a dress or a pair of shoes, and you have carefully planned your budget, buy it! The same principle holds true if your electric bill is past due and you want to go on a trip, don't do it. Be a sound decision maker. Base your decisions on your current financial picture and not on what you desire. Balance your checkbook after every purchase. Review your current financial picture on a weekly, monthly, and quarterly basis. If you don't like what you see, change it.

Help others achieve their goals in life.

You may have heard that "if you help others get what they want, you will get want you want. I believe in helping others. I feel we are blessed by the number of people we help to achieve their goals in life. Don't worry that you might not have enough food for your own family, when you are helping, there will always be plenty to go around.

Seek wisdom and lead with confidence and dignity.

Educate yourself and become the best in your chosen field. Have confidence in your ability to make decisions based on knowledge and facts. Lead with dignity and strength, and be assured your actions will not bring harm to you personally, or to your family.

Let your works bring you praise.

Your children will rise up and bless you for a job well done. Your husband will be known as a respected man. Work hard on your job, work hard on keeping yourself beautiful, but work harder at raising your children and protecting the future of your family.

How to Focus on the Finished Products

In business, we are rated on results. We are considered a success if the bottom line for the company has increased, based on our productivity. What is your customer satisfaction rating? How well are you training and managing your employees. In our homes, we are rated by our children or spouse. We are judged on how well we manage our time and relationships with our family. We must focus our energy on the final and finished products to be successful women.

Focus on the end results for your children.

How well have you trained your children? Can the girls cook or keep the house neat and clean. Have the boys been trained to take out the trash or mow the lawn. As working women, often we are caught being too tired to train our children to be independent. We forget they will someday leave our home and have to manage their own homes and families. Are you training and preparing for the end results. If not, start now.

In my home, my children have assigned duties. The girls take turns washing the dishes or washing the clothes. My son is the living room boy or the trash man. Teaching them to be responsible and to take care of their home will make them effective workers outside of the home. I believe in training for independence.

The Bible says "Train up a child the way he should go and he will not depart from it" (Proverbs 22:6 NKJV). If we want kids who will be productive in life, we must start now by teaching them to be responsible.

Focus on the relationship between you and your spouse.

One weekend, our kids went to their friend's house to spend the night. My husband and I were left at home. We found ourselves not having much to say or do without the kids. I realized at that moment that soon this would be the reality of our lives. If we don't focus on our relationship now, we will have no relationship when they are gone.

I began immediately to take steps to assure we had a quality relationship with each other. I planned a romantic evening for just the two of us. We both agreed we would not talk about the kids or past mistakes. We simply focused on now and the future. We had such a great time together; I had almost forgotten how much I enjoyed his company.

Steps to Successfully Fulfilling Your Life's Passion

Becoming a teacher has always been one of my passions. I was advised that there was no money in teaching, so I followed the advice of my parents and peers and majored in real estate investment and analysis. Although I have no regrets about my career choice, my passion was to become a teacher.

Everything I do now is geared toward education and giving instruction to others. I have sold real estate and provided financing for hundreds of customers, and educated and trained all of my employees. My passion was to become an educator, and finally, I am able to realize that dream.

You will know your passion in life if you are willing to do it for free! If you wake up every day and dream of doing something and you don't follow through with your heart's desire, you will begin to feel unfulfilled.

When I turned forty, I realized that I still had passions unfulfilled. I had the passion to become an educator, author, and public speaker. I wanted to open a real estate and mortgage school to educate and train individuals on becoming successful within the mortgage and real estate industry. I began pursuing my dreams by writing several books and manuals for real estate professionals.

Five Steps to Successfully Fulfilling Your Passion

- Recognize and write down your passion.

The first step in fulfilling your passion is to understand what you want out of life. It must be visual. It must be specific in nature. It must be realistic.

- Develop a plan to implement your goal.

A plan requires action steps. Write down the action steps required to reach your goals.

- Set a timeline for events to happen that will bring you closer to your passion.

Develop a time-line for your plan to be effective, and use it to measure your effectiveness. If you realize you are not on target according to the plan reorganize it.

- Evaluate your effectiveness.

Schedule a weekly meeting with yourself. Look at your written plan, measure the timeline you set for yourself. Review and analyze your current position. Make sure you are on target.

- Celebrate your success.

Finally, the date has come and it is time to celebrate your success. Throw a big party for yourself. Invite your friends to celebrate your success.

About the Author

Tunita R. Bailey is native of Dallas, Texas. She graduated from David W. Carter High School in 1982, and continued her studies at the University of North Texas, where she graduated with a bachelor's in Business Administration with emphasis in Real Estate Investment and Analysis.

Ms. Bailey obtained her real estate license in 1986, and worked as a real estate agent and property manager, overseeing a multi-million dollar residential and commercial portfolio for a leading real estate company. In 1993, she joined a nationwide mortgage banking firm, where she received training and excelled as a top-producing loan officer.

In 1995, Ms. Bailey left banking and joined a mortgage brokerage firm as a sales manager. After a few months, she formed a new mortgage brokerage firm, Creative Mortgage Lending Corporation, and it quickly excelled to one of the largest minority-woman owned and operated brokerage firms in the southwest sector of Dallas. As president/CEO, Ms. Bailey was responsible for recruiting, managing, and training several loan officers and processors to become mortgage professionals.

After seventeen years as a mortgage and real estate broker/owner and certified trainer, she is now author of Mortgages: Bringing Success Home, and has created workbooks, reference manuals, and training materials for professionals in the mortgage brokerage and real estate industry.

For more information, contact Tunita at 214-793-4831, or e-mail her at tunitabailey@sbcglobal.net.

www.todaysmortgageexpert.net

Chapter 17

A River Reaches Places Its Source Never Knows

BRYAN FLANAGAN

Where does *inspiration* come from? Where do you find your inspiration? Where do you go when you want or need to be inspired?

If you make yourself available for inspiration, you will find it all around you. You will also find the people who inspire you the most, often do not realize they serve as inspiration.

Oswald Chambers has touched countless lives for nearly a century. His talent, his heart, his spirit, and his love for God continue to inspire, even though he passed away in 1917. Mr. Chambers' daily devotional book, *My Utmost for His Highest*, has been in the top ten titles of Christian books since its release in the United States in 1935. With millions of copies in print, it is a Christian classic.

Oswald Chambers was born in 1874 in Aberdeen, Scotland. While a teenage, he was converted to Christianity under the ministry of Charles Haddon Spurgeon. After studying theology, Chambers traveled as an itinerant Bible teacher in the United States, Japan, and the United Kingdom. In 1911, he founded the Bible Training College in Clapham, London. The school was closed in 1915 due to World War I. Shortly thereafter, he and his wife sailed for Egypt, where he served as a YMCA chaplain. He also ministered to the troops from New Zealand and Australia who were guarding the Suez Canal.

Chambers died in 1917, following surgery for a ruptured appendix. His wife of seven years, Gertrude, a trained court stenographer, compiled his messages and sermons and published *My Utmost for His Highest* in 1927. It is the best-selling devotional of all time.

Chambers continues to inspire people nearly one hundred years after his death. Yet, he did not intend to inspire people in the twenty-first century. He was simply sharing his talent, his heart, his spirit, and his love for God with those who needed it. His intention was not to inspire. His intention was to share God's truth, and to be obedient to God's will in his life. Yet he continues to inspire.

He addresses this in the message of May 18. I am paraphrasing a bit, but this is his essential message:

We often impair God's designed inspiration, which He desires to exhibit through us, because of our own conscious efforts to be consistent and useful. Jesus says there is only one way to develop and grow spiritually, and that is through focusing and concentrating on God. In essence, Jesus was saying, "Don't worry about inspiring others; simply believe on Me."

The people who inspire us the most are not those who detain us with continual talk, but those who live their lives like the stars in the sky and "the lilies of the field"—simply and unaffected. Those are the lives that mold, shape, and inspire us.

He then makes his point again in his message on September 6 by stating, "A river reaches places which its source never knows." That sentence inspires me even as it illustrates precisely how inspiration works. We are touched and inspired by people who have no idea they have inspired us. What a great gift to possess, to be able to touch people with no ego involved!

I would like to share some examples of people who continue to inspire, who continue to reach places of which they aren't aware. You will recognize some people, and you will not recognize others. Yet, they are all truly, "lilies of the field."

Inspired by a Quiet Confidence

I met my best friend the first day of seventh grade. I was a nervous junior high school student. Yet, Ralph Watts was different. He had his act together before the rest of us. We all envied his quiet confidence. Ralph was mature beyond his years. He was a dreamer. Because he was raised by a single mom, he went to work before the rest of us. He still managed to play sports, involve himself in extracurricular activities, and maintain a very busy social calendar but he had it rougher than the rest of us in both his home life, and finances. Ralph, however, had a faith in himself, a self-belief that was grounded deeply in his soul. At times, his grades suffered, as did his attention to school assignments. When the guidance counselor suggested he go to a vocational school and skip college, Ralph just laughed. You see, Ralph didn't believe in guidance counselors; he believed in himself.

After Ralph graduated with two master's degrees, he went on to a very successful career as a hospital administrator in New Orleans, Louisiana. When I asked him how he had moved all the way to the top of his profession, he smiled and said: "I've never stopped dreaming big. The problem with a lot of my associates in the healthcare profession, is that they stopped dreaming big. Somewhere along the line, they must have lost faith in themselves and stopped dreaming big. It's sad."

We buried Ralph on Good Friday in 1998. You should have seen the people who attended his funeral. They came from all over—from Pennsylvania, to California, to Australia. You see, Ralph Watts inspired all those he met. However, his intent was not to be an inspiration to people. His intent was to share his quiet confidence with you. When you left a meeting with him, you felt better than when you began the meeting.

My friendship with Ralph extended thirty-eight years. I miss him every day, he continues to inspire me.

Inspired by a Positive Attitude

My wife and I have been married for thirty-six years. And it's been the best twenty-nine years of her life! Just teasing, Cyndi!

Cyndi's roommate in college was Molly Clark. They were as close as sisters, and consequently, I become very close to Molly. One year after graduation, Molly lost her sight to diabetes. What a tragic thing to happen to a beautiful, intelligent, faith-based young lady. Well, that's what we thought. That's what her friends thought. Cyndi was closer to Molly than most of us, and she made this statement: "Just wait to you see what Molly does with this blindness."

You see, Molly could have gotten bitter, but she didn't. She got better. Her attitude was: God gave me this for a reason, and I am going to honor Him. So, she enrolled at the Bible Institute of Los Angeles and earned a master's degree in Family Counseling. When Cyndi and I visited Molly in Los Angeles while she was in school, we discovered that she was touching lives all over the world. The previous summer, she had toured most of the world with a Christian song and praise worship team. Our visit was cut short because Molly had an emergency. It seems that one of her close friends was experiencing trouble in her marriage. So, Molly had made reservations to fly to Alabama to support her friend. When we asked who was accompanying her on the trip, she smiled and said, "God and I are enough for this trip."

Today, Molly is married, and she still maintains a private counseling practice in North Louisiana. Molly continues to inspire people with her actions and her positive outlook.

Inspired by Learning

Harry Chase is a hero to me in every sense of the word.

He joined the US Navy in 1936. Nothing unusual about that, except Harry was just sixteen years old when his parents allowed him to enlist. As the oldest of seven children, Harry thought it was time to strike out on his own. He had no high school degree, he was unchurched, and he was searching for a direction in his life. And yet, over the next seventy years, Harry achieved a degree of success few of us realize.

In 1940, Harry was in San Diego, California, when he met his future wife, Mary Ellen, at a social event at a Presbyterian Church. One year later, while stationed in Hawaii, Harry heard God call him into the ministry. Mary Ellen and Harry were excited about the direction they were about to take. They had decided they would serve the Lord once Harry's service to his country was concluded. They planned how they were going to achieve their dream and answer God's call. While Mary Ellen taught school, Harry would use the GI Bill to fund his college education.

The year was 1941. Harry was to conduct his very first Sunday school lesson on Sunday, December 7, 1941. At 7:45 a.m., while waiting on ship to be ferried to shore, he noticed several unfamiliar planes flying toward Pearl Harbor. Harry was a bit upset that World War II was keeping him from being a minister. He had many talks with God about this delay in his path to becoming a reverend.

Once the war concluded, Harry received a degree from San Diego Statek, and went on to Princeton Theological Seminary, where he graduated with honors. He served as college chaplain for ten years before pastoring several churches. Upon retirement, he moved to Plano, Texas, and became a teacher and liturgist at my church. He continued to reach people by teaching at a local community college. His subjects ranged from resolving family conflicts, to his personal favorite, how to read the Bible.

I attended his adult Sunday school class for six years. His lessons were more of an experience than a lecture, as Harry had a talent to involve each and every member of the class. All of us would share the lessons with our family, friends, and business associates the following week. Harry taught, he inspired, and he loved his class into growing spiritually.

Each of his lessons contained golden nuggets of truth and inspiration. Let me share some of these with you:

Christianity should be fun.

The secular world will stand in amazement.

Christianity is one beggar telling another beggar about bread.

If I have the authority to revise the Bible, then the Bible has no authority.

Don't sell prayer short.

I thought the events in the Bible took as long to happen as it did for me to read about them!

Continue to be a Christian this week. Just do it a little better than last week.

Whoever tells the stories, shapes the culture. But you must know the story!

I love Harry Chase. I once told my wife that the next time it floods I want to stand next to Harry Chase because Harry stands on a little higher ground than the rest of us.

Harry was an inspiration even to many people who have not met him. He was truly a river that touched places he never knew.

Let me leave you with this thought, one of the golden nuggets Harry shared with me: When you are born, you cry, and others rejoice. Live your life so that when you die, others cry, and you rejoice.

About the Author

Bryan began his career as a delivery boy for the IBM Corporation in Baton Rouge. He then invested the next fourteen years with IBM as a salesman, a "people" manager, and a sales instructor at IBM's national training center. In 1984, Bryan joined the Zig Ziglar Corporation in Dallas, Texas. For the next twenty years, he served clients in a variety of industries, ranging from professional services, to high tech, to pharmaceutical companies.

In 2005, Bryan founded Flanagan Training Group. In this capacity, he designs and delivers training programs that improve team and individual productivity and growth.

He understands what is required to achieve success in today's competitive environment.

Let Bryan put his real-world experience to work for you and your team. One thing you can count on: Bryan has fun during his presentation—and so do his audiences.

You'll laugh as you learn!!!

For more information please, visit www.flanagantraining.com.

Chapter 18

Navigating Life Circumstances
* You Are the Navigator

MICHELLE MILLER

Many of us are so burdened by life circumstances, that we have effectively abandoned our inherent role as navigators. We thus relegate ourselves to rickety vessels, and are unwittingly tossed around by whatever weather conditions life presents. In so doing, we live a life in miniature. We travel life's potentially picturesque journey with a small image of ourselves, along the way questioning our ability to master control of our lives. We find ourselves drifting with the currents, instead of boldly charting the course of our destinies. This miniature image of self, created by fear, persuades us to surrender our authenticity and to live a life of anguish and despair, allowing our dreams and aspirations to remain dormant.

Our lives need not be so.

Such a doldrums-driven approach to living is limiting, preventing us from achieving our true desires. To break from this cycle of self-minimization, we must ask—and honestly answer—the truly big question of who we really believe ourselves to be. We then must find the courage to broaden our perception of self, the first step in resuming our rightful place as navigator of our own lives.

The word 'navigator' is defined as: ". . . the person onboard a ship or aircraft responsible for the navigation of the vessel. The navigator's responsibilities include planning the journey, advising while en route, and ensuring that hazards or obstacles are avoided." (http://en.wikipedia.org/wiki/Navigator)

Essentially, you are your life's navigator, the sole person in charge of making sure you are traveling in the right direction. Your ability to expand your belief of who you are will better enable you to discern your life's purpose, and to confidently navigate your life circumstances.

Navigating Principles

The following are fundamental principles for a successful life voyage:

1. Possess an earnest appreciation of who you are.

2. Comprehend the structural design of your vessel.

3. Discern the purpose for which you travel.

Through the lens of imagination, we can explore a colorful analogy that challenges our understanding of who we think we are, focusing on these three navigating principles. To completely embrace this intriguing expedition, however, we must be receptive to the idea that the totality of who we really are is spirit.

Imagine that life is an infinite, all-inclusive, ever-flowing waterway, purposely created for an exhilarating journey. This perfectly structured waterway consistently provides gratifying travel experiences with an unlimited choice of fascinating destinations. Travelers may select their ideal vessel, choose their course specifications, and determine the time they wish to arrive at selected destinations.

This incredible journey is capably facilitated through the superb vessel called the human body. If we have accepted the premise that our totality is that of spirit, then it follows that the body is but a mere fraction of our essence. This is not to suggest that the body is insignificant, as it is a majestic creation. The human body is impeccably designed, and soundly engineered for our amazing journeys. Indeed, the body as a vessel for our life travels is a profound concept; each vessel is uniquely designed with striking external features. However, the most crucial aspect of our vessels lies in the powerful control devices housed within. Each of us is fully equipped with particular essentials needed for the selected travel.

This provocative concept is beautifully validated by the fact that we are created in the image and after the likeness of the master Creator. But despite our impressive pedigree, we nevertheless have somehow lost our authentic identity, and our innate ability to successfully navigate our lives. Consequently, today, this open waterway has been reduced for us, and by us, to an intolerant fast lane, jammed with the traffic of anxiety, the curves of chaos, the bottlenecks of confusion, and the detours of despair and frustration. This apparently organized chaos and turmoil is what we have come to accept as the reality of daily living. But true navigators are always in control; notice that ship captains, plane pilots, and car drivers are fully aware they are in complete control, possessing the essential apparatus to skillfully navigate their course. True navigators are not merely swept along by currents, but active charters of their own course, regardless of the weather.

So it should be, and can be for you. Regardless of what obstacles and hazards life presents, you are the navigator, and you can effectively chart your own life course.

Let's now explore these organizing principles in more detail as a means of helping us unlock the navigator within.

Awareness of Who You Are

Possess an earnest appreciation of who you are.

Acceptance and appreciation of yourself, just as you are, is the first fundamental principle, and it is critically essential. It can also be one of the most difficult principles to master, given our social climate, and popular culture's embrace of a shallow, celebrity-driven ideal.

Indeed, in a world of materialism and obsession with "celebrity identity," the idea that we are more than mere physical beings is not readily accepted. Hence, natural, innate characteristics, such as courage, faith, and determination, are overshadowed by shallow dependency on designer labels and other "success" symbols.

Our apparent obsession with entertainment in general, and "celebrity identity" in particular, is now endemic. The mass media generously feeds this crazed addiction with a barrage of programs that idolize fame and fortune. As a result, ordinary people are unable to perceive the totality of who they really are beyond the images they see on television screens, computer monitors, magazines, or daily news papers. The simple fact is that most of us cannot possibly "measure up" to the idealized glamour of our celebrities, and our concept of self becomes stilted and limiting. We are not Brad Pitt. We are not Angelina Jolie. We are not celebrities, and it seems the best we can hope for is to adopt the brands and mannerisms of our celebrities in a desperate attempt to be what we patently are not. And so intricate details of who we believe ourselves to be are cultivated based on a deceptive reality. This invariably serves only to keep us focused on what we do not have as opposed to honoring that which we do.

Certainly, there is a role for entertainment, and there may be positive aspects of celebrities, or those we consider role models, that we might wish to emulate. After all, the fact that Bono is a celebrity in no way diminishes his efforts on behalf of AIDS victims; indeed, without his celebrity status, his efforts would not be nearly as effective.

That having been said, our objective must be to add value to who we already are, not to establish our identity by yearning to be someone else. The more fascinating point in the advertising slogan, "I want to be like Mike," was that Michael Jordan also wanted to be like Mike. The true power of the slogan came from the fact that Jordan enjoyed being himself. When we allow ourselves to be saturated by our adoration of others to the point that we do not desire to be ourselves, we dishonor our innate greatness and the inherent value we possess. As such, we sell ourselves short, becoming overly concerned with what others think about us. But when we become too emotionally invested in what another person thinks about us, we in effect hijack our own sense of worth.

We are, each one of us, a unique creation. Authentic power is embodied within us. As such, we are all empowered to courageously navigate our lives, as we desire. The key is for us to appreciate who we are, to honor our unique authenticity. In so doing, we validate our own dreams and aspirations. Being ourselves becomes much easier when we know the remarkable individual within us.

Engineered to Move Forward

Comprehend the structural design of your vessel.

Since our totality is spirit, the body is essentially our physical means of transportation. The human body is an incredible master-piece, with one crucial specification: it is structurally engineered to consistently move forward.

Our second fundamental principle acknowledges that our bodies are specifically designed for forward motion.

The majestic power and creation of the human body is mind-boggling, a living masterpiece. We possess a profound central nervous system, and suitable external limbs engineered for consistent forward mobility, which combine to provide a marvelous vehicle for the journey of life. Examined through the prism of biology, we see that a similar, impeccable design is the nature of all living things. Creatures great and small, from grizzly bears to field mice, are gifted with the capacity to move forward. The animal kingdom is instinctively cognizant of this reality, and lives in rather orderly environments. Each creature is suitably engineered for its specific region of the planet, and blessed with the instincts to find food and shelter. In even the most unforgiving weather conditions, creatures are readily able to find sustenance.

As beings created in the image and likeness of the master Creator, however, we have a distinct advantage over other creatures. We have been given the additional gift of being born navigators. In order to utilize this gift, however, we must recognize and embrace the power embedded in our structural design. Forward motion and the powerful gift to choose give us the liberty not merely to move forward but to choose how, when, where, and why we move.

It is well worth stressing, of course, that electing not to choose is still to exercise the power of choice. As the rock group Rush put it in one song, even if we choose not to choose, we still have made a choice. And because all life's choices bring consequences, we must understand that failing to exercise our power to select a course and take our lives forward will inevitably result in our being swept forward by the currents of daily life. In such cases, we become not navigators but mere passengers in our own lives. The purpose of life, however, is to move forward with purpose—not to be swept along by soulless currents.

We are the offspring of the master Creator. Everything we need for our journey is as available to us as the rain is to the wild blades of grass in the Serengeti. The waterway of life is an abundant and very friendly place; we can obtain anything that we desire.

All that is required for us to tap into this life-giving cycle, is that we take ownership of our own power, and recognize the unlimited capacity we possess within. By recognizing and embracing our power and capacity, we may boldly and eagerly navigate our course in pursuit of our heart's desires. Just like Dorothy in *The Wizard of Oz*, we must learn that we already have everything we need to achieve our wildest dreams.

Passion-Driven Purpose

Discern the purpose for which you travel.

Life without passion is no life at all. Passion is the enthusiasm, vigor, and drive for why we do what we do. This energizing power is what makes our journey an invigorating experience, and passion derives from a sense of purpose.

Purpose is the crucial third principle for navigating life circum-stances.

Make no mistake. You are here for a great purpose. What you were born to do was carved in your heart, long before you came to know it. You embody special gifts and talents. Your goal is to find creative means to liberate your gifts and determine how they connect with your life's purpose. As the navigator, you possess the power to listen to the quietness of your heart, and unearth the incredible purpose for which you were created. Only you can play your role.

The fast-paced, boisterous environments of our lives leave very little room for us to discern our inherent qualities. As a matter of fact, we sometimes feel so swamped, that we see ourselves as powerless over our circumstances. We accept the practice of being herded off to jobs which bring a salary, but illicit no passion. Therefore, the gifted painter remains the burned-out business executive; the talented musician remains the tired waitress, and so on. What is fascinating, not to mention mind-boggling, is that this artificial style of living has become a custom. As a consequence, our manufactured careers are based primarily on where we would make the most money as opposed to where we would gain the most passion.

This money-driven approach to living produces societies decorated with tons of fabulous things, but very empty people. True happiness remains elusive. But how do we find our passion?

Each of us has something special to offer the world. The challenge for most of us is to see ourselves worthy to possess these qualities. Therefore, while following a path set by others is a novice step in the right direction, there must come a time when we define our own pathways. We must be mindful that, by virtue of birth, we have inherited innate gifts from the master Creator. To question this is to question whether the radiant color is embedded into the seed long before the flower begins to bloom.

Living a successful life is a very systematic process. All participants have an inherent role to play, and must graciously take the spotlight on schedule. You need only to trust your innate power, rise above the noise of daily living, and listen to your heart. Your purpose is congruent with who you are and how you wish to express yourself to this beautiful world.

Remind yourself that you are in control, and that you can confidently navigate your life to your desired destination.

Wrapping Up

From birth, it seems, we are taught to process life based only on what we can see with our eyes, rather than what we feel in our hearts. As such, we shape our lives solely on distorted visual aids. Those who feel they do not measure up to visual expectations tread this journey with despondent temperaments. However, the method of visually processing life is a misleading notion, because the greater part of who we are is not what we can see. Rather, the greater part of who we are is within our authenticity. As Shakespeare's Polonius put it, "To thine own self be true." It is when we are our true selves that our true greatness shines.

The notion of life as a friendly, open waterway is very liberating. Though the weather will change, and sometimes for the worse, we are each destined to experience an incredible life, free from chaos and anxiety. The only true limits we face are self-imposed. Fittingly, we must find ways to relinquish our fears, shed the skin of our circumstances, and fully embrace the waterways of our lives. It is this nurturing embrace that will provide the courage for us to reclaim our rightful place as true navigators.

Remember who you are and that, regardless of your circumstances, life is always on your side.

About the Author

Michelle Monique Miller is a proud Bahamian, living in the city of Nassau on the island of New Providence in the Bahamas. She has an insatiable appetite for life and a passion for living. The eldest of seven siblings, she has a keen appreciation for the value in being of service. She is a leader, dynamic speaker, and training facilitator. As a life coach, community builder, and executive director of Moving Forward Coaching & Training, she is committed to being an agent for positive change. This first published chapter represents the beginning of a life dream.

A twenty-year corporate professional and a Certified Compliance Specialist, Michelle has facilitated numerous training seminars and has traveled extensively. She is a certified member of the Association of Certified Anti-Money Specialists (ACAMS), a member of the Bahamas Society of Training & Development (BSTD), a member of Success University and a Board Member for the Bahamas Family Planning Association (BFPA).

Miss Michelle M. Miller
Moving Forward Coaching & Training
Web site: www.keep-moving-forward.com
Email: coach4ward@yahoo.com
Phone: {242} 477-7505

Chapter 19

Becoming a Better You

JOHNNY MORNEY

There has been an enormous amount of material developed with the idea of bringing out the greatness within us. I have personally purchased thousands of dollars-worth of products pertaining to greatness. I truly believe there is greatness in each and every one of us.

It was not always so. I had a tendency, for example, to concentrate on my past failures. I focused on my failed relationships, lost jobs, drug addiction, financial problems, illness, unrealized goals, shattered dreams, and broken promises. By sowing those seeds, I reaped low self-image, self-sabotage, self-rejection, and damaged emotions.

To top it all off, I denied that I had those traumatized emotions. Even when I admitted I had them, oftentimes I didn't like myself.

To this day, I still look for people and outside circumstances to blame for my self-hatred.

As you can imagine, it was very difficult for me to see myself as great. The "seven steps to greatness" workshops, books, tapes, and CD's seemed to be working for everyone around. Everyone but me. One day, I found the solution to my problem. I had a revelation that if I could become better, eventually I could grow to be great.

How many of you would like to be converted into a better person, mother, father, wife, or husband? Is there anyone who would like to become better at his job, better at managing his finances, or better at getting and staying physically fit? Would you like to develop into a better business leader, a better prospector?

It doesn't matter what area of your life you want to be better in. I assure you that if you take the action to get better, you can become great. However, you cannot turn out to be better or great until you learn to love yourself and take responsibility for your life.

The price of greatness is responsibility —Winston Churchill

Who Do You See When You Look in the Mirror

The guy in the Glass

> When you get what you want in your struggle for pelf,
> And the world makes you King for a day,
> Then go to the mirror and look at yourself,
> And see what that guy has to say.
>
> For it isn't your Father, or Mother, or Wife,

Who judgment upon you must pass.
The feller whose verdict counts most in your life
Is the guy staring back from the glass.

You may be like Jack Horner and "chisel" a plum,
But the man in the glass says you're only a bum
If you can't look him straight in the eye.

He's the feller to please, never mind all the rest,
For he's with you clear up to the end,
And you've passed your most dangerous, difficult test
If the guy in the glass is your friend.
And think you're a wonderful guy,
You can fool the whole world down the pathway of years,
And get pats on the back as you pass,
But your final reward will be heartaches and tears
If you've cheated the guy in the glass.

—Dale Wimbrow, 1934

One of the things I would often do after buying drugs was to check the rearview mirror to ensure the police were not behind me. One night, I had a humbling, sobering, and liberating thing happen.

This particular time when I checked the rearview mirror, I saw the person responsible for the mess my life was in. It was me! One of the toughest challenges you'll ever face is accepting personal responsibility for your life.

As I gazed in the mirror, I didn't see any of the people, things, or circumstances I blamed for my drug use. I was the only one there.

At that point, I knew I had to take the steps to turn my life around, because no one could or would do it for me.

Once upon a time, I despised the person I saw in the mirror. All that was negative and going wrong in my life was embodied in the person in the mirror. How could the person in the mirror allow my life to spiral out of control?

I read a quote by Henry David Thoreau that changed the way I saw my situation. Thoreau said, "Things do not change; we change." At that point, I knew that if I was going to turn my life around, I would have to change the way I felt about the person in my mirror. I realized it would be up to the person in the mirror to change, and I venture to say, save, my life.

It doesn't matter how horrific your past has been, or how many mistakes you have made. Learn to love the person in the mirror because your future depends on that person.

See that person not for who he or she has been, but see him or her for whom he or she is becoming.

The only way you'll ever achieve your goals, and make your dreams come true, is to accept complete, total, 100 percent responsibility for your actions and your life.

Know Where You Are and Where You Want to Go

If you don't know where you are going, how can you expect to get there? —Basil S. Walsh

Once you take responsibility for your life, you must know where you want to go, what it is that you want to achieve. As my great friend and mentor, John Di Lemme, always says, you must find your why and fly. And then once you find your why, or your purpose in life, you must be relentless in pursuit of it.

Cynthia Kersey in her book, *Unstoppable*, mentions a survey done by prominent psychologist William Marsten. In his survey, he asked three thousand people, "What have you to live for?" Ninety-four percent responded by saying they had no definite purpose for their lives—94 percent! She went on to say "everyone dies, but not everyone really lives."

People are getting out of bed every morning without a clear direction of where they are going in life. They are like robots, just going through the motion, of a mundane daily routine. They are following someone else's agenda. Life, circumstances, and other people are forcing them in the direction they want to go.

As Ben Stein said, "The indispensable first step to getting the things you want out of life is this: decide what you want."

Stop the Blame Game

People are always blaming their circumstances for what they are. I don't believe in circumstances. The people who get on in this world are the people who get up and look for the circumstances they want, and, if they can't find them, make them. —George Bernard Shaw

I was a master at the blame game. I blamed everyone and everything, from parents who didn't raise me, to racism, to being born poor. I blamed my wife, my ex-wife, society, and my circumstances. According to me, the world was out to get me. In my mind, I was truly a helpless victim. My worldview consisted of a vast conspiracy theory. I deceived myself into believing I had every right to get high on drugs because it was the only way to relieve the pain of a cruel world.

I found out that when you blame other people and things for your condition, you give all of your power to the condition and the other people. This attitude really makes you a victim, because you don't have the power to change your situation. You have given away your power to change it. Take back your power by stopping the blame game.

I think Wayne Dyer said it best when he stated "All blame is a waste of time. No matter how much fault you find with another, and regardless of how much you blame him, it will not change you."

Take Control

Our attitudes control our lives. Attitudes are a secret power work-ing twenty-four hours a day, for good or bad. It is of paramount importance that we know how to harness and control this great force. —Tom Blandi

Your attitude is your emotional response to the adversity you encounter as you pursue your goals and use your gifts. I came to the realization that I could not always control what happened to me, but I could control how I responded to what happened to me.

When I was on drugs, I became aware of the fact that certain people and situations would trigger my involuntary use of drugs. When I was faced with those people and situations, I would go into autopilot. By realizing this, I was able to consciously take control of my thoughts and emotions, and I was able to resist the urge to use drugs.

To be successful, you must figure out who or what sneaks in and takes control of your attitudes. What, or who, is it that triggers your negative, self-debilitating thoughts? It is paramount to develop control over your thoughts, and what you say when you are faced with the storms of life. I know that's easier said than done, but you must take control.

Take control of your thoughts, because it is a proven fact that where the mind goes, the body will follow.

You Deserve It

Whatever you accomplish in life is a manifestation not so much of what you do, as of what you believe deeply within yourself that you deserve. —Les Brown

The great Les Brown is my friend and mentor. I am a member of the Les Brown Speaker's Program and Les is constantly stressing the importance of assessing yourself to see if life is giving you what you believe in your heart of hearts you deserve.

It important you know you deserve your dreams. It is not a matter of how good you are. It not a matter of how bad you have been. What matters is that you know that you were created for success.

I sometimes look back on my past life of drugs, failures, disappointments, divorce, loss of loved ones, heartache, and pain. I know that all these things happened for a reason. They were preparing me for something much greater.

The ashes in our lives are a down payment on our success. Therefore, you deserve to have your dreams. You have paid for them with more than just blood, sweat, and tears. Think about how far you've come. Think about all the obstacles and adversities you conquered.

Every time you look in the mirror, remember the person you see was born to win, and that you deserve to win.

It's Up to You

People of mediocre ability sometimes achieve outstanding success because they don't know when to quit. Most men succeed because they are determined to. —George E. Allen

If you are like I was, you are waiting for your ship to come in. I was lounging around thinking the limo driver from Successville would knock on my door, put me in the back seat of the limo and drive me to my dreams, while I did nothing.

When I was on drugs, I told myself that I wanted to quit. I prayed to God that the craving for drugs would go away. I wanted my spiritual father, the awesome Bishop T. D. Jakes, to lay hands on me to break my addiction.

My breakthrough came when I made up my mind that even if God didn't miraculously take away the cravings for drugs, and even if Bishop Jakes never laid hands on me, I still would overcome my addiction and change my life. At that point, I understood that God had already given me the victory, but it was up to me to seize it.

We all have certain God-given abilities, talents, and gifts that, once developed and properly placed, will cause us to achieve our dreams. But the sad truth of the matter is most people have yet to discover the God-given treasures that are their keys to success.

It is up to you to go out and create the world you want to live in. You have to actively participate in your journey to Successville.

The World Needs Your Gift

Our deepest fear is not that we are inadequate. Our deepest fear is that we are powerful beyond measure. It is our light, not our darkness, that most frightens us. We ask ourselves, Who am I to be brilliant, gorgeous, talented, fabulous? Actually, who are you not to be?
—Marianne Williamson

Believe it or not, you are a gift to somebody. There is someone in this world whose life may depend on you achieving your goals. Someone needs to hear your song, someone needs to read your book, and someone needs you to start that business.

Whatever your dream or goal is, there is someone in dire need of it. And I must be frank with you, someone's life may depend on you sharing your gift.

I never dreamed I would be a motivational speaker or an author. To be honest, I fought it as hard as I could. Sharing my innermost secrets and failures was the last thing I wanted to do.

As you read this, there is someone suffering, and feeling overwhelmed by issues you have already been liberated from. They desperately need to how you rose above those barriers.

By becoming all you were created to be, and sharing your gift with others, you will make the world a better place.

The Choice Is Yours

Life is truly a game of believe it or not. Regardless of whether you believe you can do something or alternatively believe you "can't," life rarely lets you down. When you believe you can—it's a sure bet that you will. On the other hand, when you think you can't—it's a cinch that you won't. Believe it or not, it's your choice. —Greg Hickman

When I hit rock-bottom, I was unemployed, my car was repossessed, my wife left me, I was nearly homeless, and to top it off, I was in a fierce battle to overcome a crack cocaine addiction. In addition, I was told that I probably had colon cancer.

At the lowest point in my life, it dawned on me that I had several options to choose from. And once I made my choice, I had to believe I could bring it to fruition. These were my options:

1. I could stay down. Staying down would mean I would give up and become a victim; basically, I could give up on life and my dreams;

2. I could get up and remain in the same place. To get up and remain in the same place would mean I would get up, but I would not advance toward my vision and dreams. I would blame others and situations for my failures. I would blame my parents because they did not raise me. I would blame my wife because she left me. I would blame society because of racism. The list goes on and on; or

3. I could get up and take a step toward my vision and dreams. I could take control of my life. I could take a step away from things I didn't want in my life, and move a step closer to the things I did want.

Ultimately, the choice was mine to make. Likewise, you have a variety of options to choose from. I made a choice to rise above my circumstances and become the person I was created to be. And let me tell you something. If I can do it, so can you!

My demon was drugs. So tell me. What is your vice, what's holding you in bondage and keeping you from your dreams? Is it fear, is it low self-esteem, is it your beliefs, is it self-pity, or is it self-sabotage?

I am here to let you know that it really doesn't matter what has held you back in the past. If you make the decision today to go after your dreams, they will come to pass.

I will leave you with this quote from Frederick Bailes. "Man's power of choice enables him to think like an angel or a devil, a king or a slave. Whatever he chooses, mind will create and manifest." The choice is yours, my friend. You are just a step away!

About the Author

Johnny Morney is an award-winning speaker and published author. As a proud member of the Les Brown Speaker's Network, he is committed to working with people who struggle with addiction, destructive behavior, or any other form of bondage that is holding them captive.

Johnny was born and raised in Houston, Texas. He earned a PhD from the School of Hard Knocks on the rough and tough streets of the 5th ward.

He knows the emotions you experience when your life is spiraling out of control, and how it feels to watch helplessly as your dreams crash and burn. There have been times in his life when success meant just hanging on.

For many years, he lived in the hell of a crack cocaine addiction. He blamed his condition on everything and everyone but the person who was truly responsible for the mess in his life.

You may be thinking "I don't have a drug problem." But Johnny will help you see that bondage is bondage, and his addiction was only a symptom of a much larger problem.

He can show you that you must get to the root cause of the issues that are really holding you in captivity, and keeping you from living the life you are dreaming of. For him, drugs were the result of his negative, self-destructive thinking. What is your obstacle or drug of choice? What is your defective thinking producing? Is it procrastination, lack of clarity and focus, self doubt, low self-esteem, fear, anger, immoral issues, sexual improprieties, uncontrolled spending, self-pity, or self sabotage? Perhaps you are struggling with why you are here and you are desperately searching for your real purpose in life.

The truth is, from time to time we all will suffer setbacks and disappointments. And we must also be willing to admit that oftentimes we are the architects of our own self demise. The setbacks and disappointments in life are not the real problem, the problem is how we deal them. It's how you deal with setbacks that will determine your success or failure in life. How you deal with adversity will also establish how long you will be held in misery.

Johnny took one step in faith, and as a result, he went from unemployed to becoming a manager on a project in Iraq worth 1.2 billion dollars. He went from dead broke to earning a six-figure salary, although he doesn't have a college degree. He went from being evicted from an apartment to building his family's dream home. My friends, Johnny went from dope to hope.

Johnny wants the world to know that it doesn't matter what you've gone through in the past, or what you are agonizing with at this moment. And as a matter of fact, it really doesn't matter how many times you've failed, the number of setbacks you've suffered, or who has hurt you.

You can rise out of the ashes of your past, and take control of the things that previously wore you down and held you in bondage!

Don't hold up your great future by dwelling on the pains of your past. Stop going around the same old mountain, take a step in faith and go northward to the promises of your divine destiny.

Johnny wants you to know that you are just a step away from your breakthrough, and the life of your dreams.

Chapter 20

Bonus Interview

WITH JACK CANFIELD

David E. Wright

Today, we are talking to Jack Canfield. You probably know him as the founder and cocreator of the *New York Times* #1 best-selling *Chicken Soup for the Soul* book series, which currently has thirty-five titles and 53 million copies in print in over thirty-two languages. Jack's background includes a BA from Harvard, a master's from the University of Massachusetts, and an Honorary Doctorate from the University of Santa Monica. He has been a high school and university teacher, a workshop facilitator, a psychotherapist, and for the past twenty-five years, a leading authority in the area of self-esteem and personal development. Jack Canfield, welcome to *Conversations on Success*!

Jack Canfield

Thank you, David. It's great to be with you.

Wright

I talked with Mark Victor Hansen a few days ago. He gave you full credit for coming up with the idea of the *Chicken Soup* series. Obviously, it's made you an internationally known personality. Other than recognition, has the series changed you personally, and if so, how?

Canfield

I would say that it has, and I think in a couple of ways. Number one, I read stories all day long of people who've overcome what would feel like insurmountable obstacles. For example, we just did a book called *Chicken Soup for the Unsinkable Soul*. There's a story in there about a single mother with three daughters. She got a disease and she had to have both of her hands and both of her feet amputated. She got prosthetic devices, and was able to learn how to use them so she could cook, drive the car, brush her daughters' hair, get a job, etc. I read that and I think, "God, what would I ever have to complain, and whine, and moan about?" So I think, at one level, it's just given me a great sense of gratitude and appreciation for everything I have—made me less irritable about the little things.

I think the other thing that's happened for me, personally, is my sphere of influence has changed. By that I mean, I got asked, for example, a couple of years ago to be the keynote speaker to the Women's Congressional Caucus and these are all the women in congress, senators, governors, and lieutenant governors in America. I said, "What do you want me to talk about, what topic?" They said, "Whatever you think we need to know to be better legislators." And I thought, "Wow, they want me to tell them about what laws they should be making and what would make a better culture?" Well, that wouldn't have happened if our books hadn't come out, and I hadn't become famous. I think I get to play with people at a higher level and have more influence in the world. That's important to me, because my life purpose is inspiring and empowering people to live their highest vision so the world works for everybody. And I get to do that on a much bigger level than when I was just a high school teacher back in Chicago.

Wright

I think one of the powerful components of that book series is that you can read a positive story in just a few minutes, then come back and revisit it. I know my daughter, who is thirteen now, has three of the books and she just reads them interchangeably. Sometimes, I go in her bedroom and she'll be crying and reading one of them. Other times, she'll be laughing—so they really are "chicken soup" for the soul, aren't they?

Canfield

They really are. In fact we have four books in the *Teenage Soul* series now, and a new one coming out at the end of this year. I was talking to one of my sons, I have a son who's eleven and he has a twelve-year-old friend who's a girl and we have a new book called *Chicken Soup for the Teenage Soul and the Tough Stuff* (It's all about dealing with parents' divorces, teachers who don't understand you, boyfriends who drink and drive, and stuff like that), and I asked her, "Why do you like this book?" because it's our most popular book among teens right now. And she said, "You know, whenever I'm feeling down, I read it, and it makes me cry, and I feel better. Some of the stories make me laugh, and some of the stories make me feel more responsible for my life. But basically, I just feel like I'm not alone." One of the people that I work with recently said that the books are like a support group between the covers of a book, to hear other peoples' experiences and realize you're not the only one going through something.

Wright

Jack, with our *Conversations on Success* publication, we're trying to encourage people in our audience to be better, to live better, and be more fulfilled by listening to the examples of our guests. Is there anything or anyone in your life who has made a difference for you and helped you to become a better person?

Canfield

Yes, and we could do ten shows just on that. I'm influenced by people all the time. If I were to go way back, I'd have to say one of the key influences in my life was Jesse Jackson, when he was still a minister in Chicago. I was teaching in an all-black high school there, and I went to Jesse Jackson's church with a friend one time. What happened for me was I saw somebody with a vision. This was before Martin Luther King was killed, and Jesse was one of the lieutenants in his organization. I just saw people trying to make the world work better for a certain segment of the population. I was inspired by that kind of visionary belief that it's possible to make change. Then later, John F. Kennedy was a hero of mine. I was very much inspired by him.

Later it was a therapist by the name of Robert Resnick that I had for two years. He taught me a little formula called E + R = O that stands for Events + Response = Outcome. He said, "If you don't like your outcomes, quit blaming the events, and start changing your responses." One of his favorite phrases was, "If the grass on the other side of the fence looks greener, start watering your own lawn more." I think it helped me get off of any kind of self-pity

I might have had because I had parents who were alcoholics and that whole number. It's very easy to blame them for your life not working. They weren't real successful or rich, and I was surrounded by people who were, and I felt like, "God, what if I'd had parents like they had? I could have been a lot better." He just got me off that whole notion, and made me realize the hand you were dealt is the hand you've got to play and take responsibility for who you are, and quit complaining and blaming others, and get on with your life. That was a turning point for me.

I'd say the last person who really affected me big-time was a guy named W. Clement Stone, who was a self-made multimillionaire in Chicago. He taught me that success is not a four-letter word, it's nothing to be ashamed of, and you ought to go for it. He said, "The best thing you can do for the poor is not be one of them." Be a model for what it is to live a successful life. So I learned from him the principles of success, and that's what I've been teaching now for the last almost thirty years.

Wright

He was the entrepreneur in the insurance industry, wasn't he?

Canfield

He was. He had combined insurance and when I worked for him he was worth 600 million dollars—and that was before the dot-com millionaires came along in Silicon Valley. He just knew more about success—and he was a good friend of Napoleon Hill, who wrote *Think and Grow Rich*—and he was a fabulous mentor. I really learned a lot from him.

Wright

I miss some of the men that I listened to when I was a young salesman coming up, and he was one of them. Napoleon Hill was another one and Dr. Peale, all of their writings made me who I am today. I'm glad that I got that opportunity.

Canfield

One speaker whose name you probably will remember, Charlie Tremendous Jones, says "Who we are is a result of the books we read and the people we hang out with." I think that's so true and that's why I tell people, "If you want to have high self-esteem, hang out with people with high self-esteem. If you want to be more spiritual, hang out with spiritual people." We're always telling our children, "Don't hang out with those kids." The reason we don't want them to is we know how influential people are with each other. I think we need to give ourselves the same advice. Who are we hanging out with? We can hang out with them in books, cassette tapes, CDs, radio shows like yours, and in person.

Wright

One of my favorites was a fellow named Bill Gove from Florida. I talked with him about three or four years ago, and he's retired now. His mind is still as quick as it ever was. I thought he was one of the greatest speakers I had ever heard.

What do you think makes up a great mentor. In other words, are there characteristics that mentors seem to have in common?

Canfield

I think there are two obvious ones. One, I think they have to have the time to do it, and two, the willingness to do it. And then three, I think they need to be someone who is doing something you want to do. W. Clement Stone used to tell me, "If you want to be rich, hang out with rich people. Watch what they do, eat what they eat, dress the way they dress. Try it on." It wasn't like give up your authentic self, but it was that they probably have habits that you don't have. Study them, study the people who are already like you.

I always ask salespeople in an organization, "Who are the top two or three in your organization?" I tell them to start taking them out to lunch and dinner and for a drink and finding out what they do. Ask them, "What's your secret?" Nine times out of ten they'll be willing to tell you. It goes back to what we said earlier about asking. I'll go into corporations and I'll say, "Who are the top ten people?" They'll all tell me and I'll say, "Did you ever ask them what they do different than you?" They go, "No." "Why not?" "Well they might not want to tell me." "How do you know? Did you ever ask them? All they can do is say no. You'll be no worse off than you are now."

So I think with mentors, you just look at people who seem to be living the life you want to live, achieving the results you want to achieve. And then, what we tell them in our book is when you approach a mentor, they're probably busy and successful, and so they haven't got a lot of time. Just say, "Can I talk to you for ten minutes every month?" If I know it's only going to be ten minutes, I'll probably say yes. The neat thing is if I like you, I'll always give you more than ten minutes, but that ten minutes gets me in the door.

Wright

In the future, are there any more Jack Canfield books authored singularly?

Canfield

Yes, I'm working on two books right now. One's called $E + R = O$ which is that little formula I told you about earlier. I just feel I want to get that out there, because every time I give a speech, when I talk about that the whole room gets so that you could hear a pin drop, it gets silent. You can tell that people are really getting value. Then, I'm going to do a series of books on the principles of success. I've got about one hundred fifty of them that I've identified over the years. I have a book down the road I want to do that's called *No More Put-Downs* which is a book probably aimed mostly at parents, teacher, and managers. There's a culture we have now of put-down humor, whether it's *Married With Children* or *All in the Family*, there's that characteristic of macho put-down humor. There's research now that's showing how bad it is for kids' self-esteem, coworkers, and athletes when the coaches do it, so I want to get that message out there as well.

Wright

It's really not that funny, is it?

Canfield

No, we'll laugh it off because we don't want to look like we're a wimp, but underneath we're hurt. The research now shows that you're better off breaking a child's bones than you are breaking their spirit. A bone will heal much more quickly than their emotional spirit will.

Wright

I remember recently reading a survey where people listed the top five people who had influenced them in their lives. I've tried it on a couple of groups at church and other places. In my case, and also in the survey, it's running that about three out of the top five are always teachers. I wonder if that's going to be the same in the next decade.

Canfield

I think that's probably because, as children, we're at our most formative years. We actually spend more time with our teachers than we do with our parents. Research shows that the average parent . . . interacts verbally with each of their children only about eight and a half minutes a day. Yet, at school, you're interacting with your teacher for anywhere from six to eight hours, depending on how long your school day is, and coaches, chorus directors, and all that kind of thing.

So, I think that, in almost everybody's life, there's been that one teacher who loved you as a human being, and not just a subject matter, some person they were supposed to fill full of history and English. And that person believed in you and inspired you. Les Brown is one of the great motivational speakers in the world. If it hadn't been for one teacher who said, "I think you can do more than be in a special ed class; I think you're the one," he'd probably still be cutting grass in the median strip of the highways in Florida instead of being a $35,000-a-talk speaker.

Wright

I had a conversation one time with Les when he was talking about this wonderful teacher who discovered that he was dyslexic. Everybody else called him dumb, and this one lady just took him under her wing and had him tested. His entire life changed because of her interest in him.

Canfield

I'm on the board of advisors of the Dyslexic Awareness Resource Center here in Santa Barbara. The reason is I taught high school with a lot of kids who were called "at-risk," kids who would end up in gangs and so forth. What we found, over and over, was that about 78 percent of all the kids in the juvenile detention centers in Chicago were kids who had learning disabilities, primarily dyslexia, but there were others as well. They were never diagnosed, and they weren't doing well in school, so they'd drop out. As soon as you drop out of school, you become subject to the influence of gangs and other kinds of criminal and drug linked activities. If they had just diagnosed these kids earlier, and there are a lot of really good programs that can teach dyslexics to read and so forth, then we'd get rid of half of the juvenile crime in America.

Wright

My wife is a teacher, and she brings home stories that are heartbreaking, about parents not being as concerned about their children as they used to be, or at least not as helpful as they used to be. Did you find that to be a problem when you were teaching?

Canfield

It depends on what kind of district you're in. If it's a poor district, the parents could be drugged out, on alcohol, not available, basically. If you're in a really high-rent district, the parents are not . . . available because they're both working, coming home tired, they're jet-setters, they're working late at the office because they're workaholics. Sometimes, it just legitimately takes two paychecks to pay the rent anymore. I find that the majority of parents care, but often they don't know what to do. They don't know how to discipline their children. They don't know how to help them with their homework. They're not passing on skills that they never got.

Unfortunately, the trend tends to be like a chain letter. The people with the least amount of skills tend to have the most number of children. The other thing is you get crack babies. In Los Angeles, one out of every ten babies born is a crack baby.

Wright

That's unbelievable.

Canfield

Yes, and another statistic is 50 percent of kids, by the time they're twelve years old, have started experimenting with alcohol. I see a lot of that in the Bible Belt. It's not the big city, urban designer drugs, but you get a lot of alcoholism. Another thing you get, unfortunately, is a lot of, let's call it 'familial violence'—a lot of kids getting beat up and hit, parents who drink and then explode. And, as we talked about earlier, child abuse and sexual abuse. You see a lot of that.

Wright

Most people are fascinated by these TV shows about being a survivor. What has been the greatest comeback that you have made from adversity in your career or in your life.

Canfield

You know, it's funny, I don't think I've had a lot of major failures and setbacks where I had to start over. My life's been kind of on an intentional curve. But I do have a lot of challenges. Mark and I are always setting goals that challenge us, and we always say, "The purpose of setting a really big goal is not so that you can achieve it so much, but it's who you become in the process of achieving it."

A friend of mine, Jim Rose, says, "You want to set goals big enough, so that in the process of achieving them, you become someone worth being." I think that to be a millionaire is nice, but so what? People make the money, they lose it. People get the big houses, and they burn down or Silicon Valley goes belly-up, and all of a sudden, they don't have a big house anymore. But who you became in the process of learning how to do that can never be taken away from you. So what we do is we constantly put big challenges in front of us. Right now, we have a book coming out in a month called *Chicken Soup for the Teacher's Soul*. You'll have to make sure to get a copy for your wife. I was a teacher and I was a teacher trainer for years. But in the last seven years, because of the success of the *Chicken Soup* books, I haven't been in the education world that much. So I've got to go out and relearn How do I market to that world? I met with a superintendent of schools. I met with a guy named Jason Dorsey who's one of the number one consultants in the world in that area. I found out who has the best-selling book in that area. I sat down with his wife for a day and talked about her marketing approaches.

So I believe that if you face any kind of adversity, whether it's you lose your job, your husband dies, you get divorced, you're in an accident like Christopher Reeve and become paralyzed, or whatever, you simply do what you have to do. You find out who's already handled this and how did they do it. Then, you find out either from their book, or from their tape, or by talking to them, or interviewing them, and you get the support you need to get through it. Whether it's a counselor in your church or you go on a retreat or you read the Bible. You do something that gives you the support you need to get to the other end and you have to know what the end is that you want to have.

Do you want to be remarried? Do you just want to have a job and be a single mom? What is it? If you reach out and ask for support, I think people really like to help other people. They're not always available, because sometimes they're going through it. But there's always someone with a helping hand. Often, I think we let our pride get in the way. We let our stubbornness get in the way. We let our belief in how the world should be get in our way, instead of dealing with how the world is. When we get that out of that way, then we can start doing that which we need to do to get where we need to go.

Wright

If you could have a platform and tell our audience something that you feel would help or encourage them, what would you say?

Canfield

I'd say number one, believe in yourself, and believe in your dreams, and trust your feelings. I think too many people are trained like when they're little kids and they're mad at their daddy, they're told, "You're not mad at your daddy." They go, "Gee, I thought I was." Or you say, "That's going to hurt." The doctor says, "No it's not." Then they give you the shot, and it hurts. They say, "See that didn't hurt, did it?" You start not to trust yourself. Or you say to your mom, "Are you upset?" and your mom says, "No," when she really is. So you stop learning to trust your perception.

I tell the story over and over there are hundreds of people I've met who've come from upper-class families where they make big incomes and the dad's a doctor, and the kid wants to be a mechanic and work in an auto shop because that's what he loves. The family says, "That's beneath us. You can't do that." So the kid ends up being an anesthesiologist killing three people because he's not paying attention. What he really wants to do is tinker with cars.

I tell people, you've got to trust your own feelings, your own motivations, what turns you on, what you want to do, what makes you feel good, and quit worrying about what other people say, think, want for you. Decide what you want for yourself, and then do what you need to do to go about getting it. It takes work. I always tell people that I read a book a week, minimum, and at the end of the year I've read fifty-two books. We're talking about professional books, books on self-help, finances, psychology, parenting, and so forth. At the end of ten years, you've read 520 books. That puts you in the top 1 percent of people knowing stuff in this country. But most people are spending their time watching TV.

W. Clement Stone told me when I went to work for him, "I want you to cut out one hour a day of TV." I said, "OK, what do I do with it?" He said, "Read." He told me what kind of stuff to read. He said, "At the end of a year you'll have spent 365 hours reading. Divide that by a forty-hour work week, and that's nine and half weeks of education every year." I thought, "Wow, that's two months." It's like going back to summer school. As a result of that, I have close to wight thousand books in my library. The reason I'm on your show instead of someone else, is that people like me, and Jim Rohn, and Les Brown, and you, read a lot. We listen to tapes and we go to those seminars. That's why we're the people with the information. I always say that your raise becomes effective when you do. You'll become more effective as you gain more skills, more insight, and more knowledge.

Wright

Jack, I have watched your career for over a decade, and your accomplishments are just outstanding. But your humanitarian efforts are really what impress me. I think that you're doing great things, not only in California, but all over the country.

Canfield

It's true. In addition to all of the work we do, we have all of our books. We pick one to three charities, and we've given away over six million dollars in the last eight years, along with our publisher, who matches every penny we give away. We've planted over a million trees in Yosemite National Park. We've bought hundreds of thousands of cataract operations in third-world countries. We've contributed to the Red Cross, the Humane Society, and on it goes. It feels like a real blessing to be able to make that kind of a contribution in the world.

Wright

Today we have been talking to Jack Canfield, the founder and cocreator of the *Chicken Soup for the Soul* book series, which currently has thirty-five titles, and I'll have to update this. It was 53 million. How many has it been now, Jack?

Canfield

We're almost up to 78 million. We have a book coming out in just a couple of weeks called *Chicken Soup for the Soul of America*. It's all stories that grew out of September 11, and it's a real healing book for our nation. I would encourage your listeners to get themselves a copy and share it with their families.

Wright

I will stand in line to get one of those. Thank you so much being with us on *Conversations on Success*.

About the Author

Jack Canfield is one of America's leading experts on developing self-esteem and peak performance. A dynamic and entertaining speaker, as well as a highly sought-after trainer, he has a wonderful ability to inform and inspire audiences toward developing their own human potential and personal effectiveness.

Jack Canfield is most well-known for the *Chicken Soup for the Soul* book series, which he coauthored with Mark Victor Hansen, and for his audio programs about building high self-esteem. Jack is the founder of Self-Esteem Seminars, located in Santa

Multiple Streams of Inspiration

Barbara, California, which trains entrepreneurs, educators, corporate leaders, and employees how to accelerate the achievement of their personal and professional goals. Jack is also the founder of The Foundation for Self-Esteem, located in Culver City, California, which provides self-esteem resources and training to social workers, welfare recipients, and human resource professionals.

Jack graduated from Harvard in 1966, received his MEd. degree at the University of Massachusetts in 1973, and an honorary doctorate from the University of Santa Monica. He has been a high school and university teacher, a workshop facilitator, a psychotherapist, and for the past thirty years, a leading authority in the area of self-esteem and personal development.

As a result of his work with prisoners, welfare recipients, and inner-city youth, Jack was appointed by the state legislature to the California Task Force to Promote Self-Esteem and Personal and Social Responsibility. He also served on the board of trustees of the National Council for Self-Esteem.

Jack Canfield
P.O. Box 30880
Santa Barbara, CA 93130
E-mail: info4jack@jackcanfield.com